Retail Sales Book!

Laurel D. Malvern

Copyright © 2024 by Laurel D. Malvern

All rights reserved. No part of this book may be reproduced, stored in a retrieval system, or transmitted in any form or by any means, electronic, mechanical, photocopying, recording, scanning, or otherwise, without the prior written permission of the publisher, except as permitted under the Copyright Act of 1976.

The information contained in this book is for educational and informational purposes only. It is not intended as a substitute for professional advice, guidance, or training in the field of retail sales. The author and publisher disclaim any liability for any loss or damage incurred by individuals or organizations as a result of reliance on information contained in this book.

While every effort has been made to ensure the accuracy and completeness of the information presented in this book, the author and publisher make no representations or warranties of any kind, express or implied, about the completeness, accuracy, reliability, suitability, or availability with respect to the information, products, services, or related graphics contained in this book for any purpose. Any reliance you place on such information is therefore strictly at your own risk.

The mention of specific companies, products, or services in this book does not imply endorsement or recommendation by the author or publisher. Views expressed by individuals or organizations in this book are their own and do not necessarily reflect the views of the author or publisher.

Any trademarks, service marks, product names, or company names mentioned in this book are used for identification purposes only and belong to their respective owners.

For permissions or inquiries regarding the use of content from this book, please contact the publisher.

"Retail Sales Book"

Preface 8

Chapter Introduction: Welcome to the World of Retail Sales 11

Chapter: Brief Overview of the Retail Industry 13

Chapter: Importance of Retail Sales in Business Success 16

Chapter: Introducing the Retail Sales Book: Your Ultimate Guide to Excelling in Retail 20

Chapter: Understanding the Retail Landscape 23

Chapter: Evolution of Retail: From Brick-and-Mortar to Omnichannel 26

Chapter: Key Players in the Retail Industry 29

Chapter: Current Trends and Future Projections 32

Chapter: The Impact of Technology on Retail Sales 36

Chapter: The Psychology of Selling 39

Chapter: Understanding Consumer Behavior 42

Chapter: Principles of Persuasion and Influence 45

Chapter: Building Trust and Rapport with Customers 48

Chapter: Overcoming Objections and Handling Rejections 51

Chapter: Mastering Product Knowledge 54

Chapter: Importance of Product Knowledge in Retail Sales 57

- Chapter: Strategies for Learning and Retaining Product Information 60
- Chapter: How to Tailor Product Knowledge to Different Customer Segments 63
- Chapter: Leveraging Product Knowledge to Upsell and Cross-Sell 67
- Chapter: Effective Communication Skills 70
- Chapter: The Power of Effective Communication in Retail Sales 73
- Chapter: Verbal and Nonverbal Communication Techniques 76
- Chapter: Active Listening and Asking Powerful Questions 79
- Chapter: Handling Difficult Customers with Grace and Professionalism 82
- Chapter: The Art of Selling Techniques 85
- Chapter: The Sales Process: From Greeting to Closing 88
- Chapter: Feature-Benefit Selling: Highlighting Product Value 91
- Chapter: Creating Irresistible Offers and Promotions 94
- Chapter: Creating Irresistible Offers and Promotions 97
- Chapter: Techniques for Closing Sales and Securing Customer Loyalty 100
- Chapter: Providing Exceptional Customer Service 103
- Chapter: Understanding the Importance of Customer Service in Retail 106

Chapter: Strategies for Delivering Outstanding Customer Experiences 109

Chapter: Handling Customer Complaints and Turning Them into Opportunities 112

Chapter: Building Long-Term Relationships with Customers 115

Chapter: Harnessing the Power of Data and Analytics 118

Chapter: Introduction to Retail Analytics 121

Chapter: Using Data to Understand Customer Preferences and Behavior 124

Chapter: Implementing Data-Driven Strategies for Sales Optimization 127

Chapter: Leveraging Analytics to Forecast Trends and Improve Decision-Making 130

Chapter: Developing Your Personal Brand as a Retail Sales Professional 134

Chapter: Understanding Personal Branding and Its Relevance in Retail Sales 138

Chapter: Building Your Online Presence and Reputation 141

Chapter: Networking and Building Relationships within the Retail Industry 144

Chapter: Strategies for Career Advancement and Continued Learning 148

Conclusion: Recap of Key Concepts Covered in the Book 151

Chapter: Encouragement and Inspiration for Retail Sales Professionals 155

Chapter: Looking Ahead: Embracing Change and Continuous Improvement in Retail Sales 159

Appendix: Additional Resources for Further Learning 163

Glossary of Retail Sales Terminology 166

Preface

Welcome to the world of retail sales—a dynamic and ever-evolving landscape where opportunity and innovation collide to create endless possibilities for success. In "Retail Sales Book," I invite you on a journey of discovery, empowerment, and transformation as we explore the intricacies of the retail industry and unlock the secrets to mastering the art of sales.

Having spent years immersed in the vibrant tapestry of retail, I've witnessed firsthand the challenges and triumphs that define this exhilarating field. From the bustling corridors of brick-and-mortar stores to the virtual storefronts of the digital age, the world of retail sales is a complex ecosystem driven by consumer demand, technological advancements, and shifting market dynamics.

In this book, I've endeavored to distill my knowledge, insights, and experiences into a comprehensive guide that empowers you to navigate this terrain with confidence and finesse. Whether you're a seasoned sales professional seeking to sharpen your skills or a budding entrepreneur eager to carve out your niche in the market, "Retail Sales Book" is designed to equip you with the tools, strategies, and mindset needed to thrive in today's competitive retail landscape.

Throughout these pages, you'll discover a wealth of practical advice, actionable techniques, and real-world examples that illuminate the path to success. From understanding the psychology of selling to mastering the art of communication, from harnessing the power of data analytics to cultivating a personal brand that sets you apart, each chapter is crafted to provide you with invaluable insights and actionable takeaways that you can apply to your own journey in retail sales.

But beyond the strategies and tactics lies a deeper truth—that success in retail sales is not just about making transactions, but about building relationships, creating value, and making a meaningful difference in the lives of your customers. It's about embodying the principles of integrity, empathy, and professionalism that elevate the sales experience from transactional to transformational.

As you embark on this journey, I encourage you to approach each chapter with an open mind and a spirit of curiosity. Allow yourself to embrace the challenges, embrace the opportunities, and embrace the journey of growth and self-discovery that lies ahead.

Whether you're flipping through these pages in search of inspiration, guidance, or practical advice, know that you hold within your hands the keys to unlocking your full potential as a retail sales professional. May this book serve as your trusted companion, your steadfast mentor, and your guiding light as you embark on this exciting and rewarding adventure in the world of retail sales.

Here's to your success, your growth, and your mastery of the art of retail sales.

With warmest regards,

Laurel D. Malvern

Chapter Introduction: Welcome to the World of Retail Sales

Welcome to the exciting and dynamic world of retail sales! Whether you're a seasoned veteran or a newcomer eager to embark on this thrilling journey, this chapter serves as your gateway to understanding the multifaceted landscape of retail sales.

In today's interconnected global marketplace, retail sales play a pivotal role in driving economic growth and shaping consumer behavior. From the bustling storefronts of traditional brick-and-mortar establishments to the virtual storefronts of e-commerce giants, the retail industry encompasses a vast array of businesses, products, and services catering to the diverse needs and preferences of consumers worldwide.

But what exactly is retail sales, and why is it so essential to the success of businesses large and small? At its core, retail sales involve the process of selling goods or services directly to consumers for personal or household use. From the moment a customer enters a store or visits an online platform to the final transaction at the checkout counter, every interaction represents an opportunity for retailers to engage, persuade, and delight their audience.

In this chapter, we'll delve into the fundamentals of retail sales, exploring key concepts, trends, and strategies that define the industry. From understanding the importance of customer satisfaction to navigating the complexities of inventory management, we'll uncover the essential elements that drive success in retail sales.

Whether you're a sales associate working on the front lines or a business owner charting the course for your enterprise, the insights shared in this chapter will provide you with a solid foundation for navigating the ever-changing landscape of retail sales. So, buckle up and prepare to embark on an exhilarating journey into the heart of retail excellence. Welcome to the world of retail sales—where opportunity awaits at every turn.

Chapter: Brief Overview of the Retail Industry

In the vast ecosystem of commerce, few sectors rival the breadth and depth of the retail industry. From corner convenience stores to sprawling supercenters, from artisan boutiques to global e-commerce giants, retail encompasses a staggering array of businesses, each playing a unique role in meeting the diverse needs and desires of consumers.

At its essence, retail is the bridge that connects producers and manufacturers with end consumers, facilitating the exchange of goods and services in exchange for payment. This pivotal role makes retail a cornerstone of economic activity, driving consumption, employment, and innovation on a global scale.

But what exactly defines the retail industry, and how has it evolved over time? In this chapter, we'll provide a brief overview of the retail landscape, examining its history, structure, and key players.

Historical Evolution:

Retail has deep roots in human history, dating back to ancient civilizations where merchants bartered goods in bustling marketplaces. Over time, the advent of currency and trade routes led to the emergence of more formalized retail systems, such as bazaars and trading posts. With the Industrial Revolution came the rise of department stores and mail-order catalogs, ushering in an era of mass consumerism and commercial expansion. In the modern era, technological advancements and globalization have transformed the retail landscape, giving rise to e-commerce platforms, omnichannel retailing, and personalized shopping experiences.

Structure of the Retail Industry:
The retail industry is characterized by a diverse array of businesses, ranging from small mom-and-pop shops to multinational corporations. These businesses operate across various sectors, including apparel, electronics, groceries, home goods, and more. Within the industry, retailers are classified based on factors such as product assortment, distribution channels, and target markets. Common retail formats include department stores, specialty stores, discount retailers, supermarkets, and online marketplaces.

Key Players:
At the heart of the retail industry are the retailers themselves—entities that buy goods from manufacturers or wholesalers and sell them to consumers for a profit. Retailers can be categorized into several tiers based on their size, scope, and market reach. Among the most prominent players in the industry are multinational corporations such as Walmart, Amazon, and Alibaba, which dominate global markets with their vast networks and economies of scale. Additionally, there are countless smaller retailers, including independent businesses, franchise operations, and online startups, each carving out its niche in the market.

Challenges and Opportunities:
While the retail industry offers boundless opportunities for growth and innovation, it also presents a myriad of challenges for businesses to navigate. From shifting consumer preferences to technological disruptions, retailers must adapt rapidly to stay competitive in a fast-paced marketplace. Additionally, factors such as supply chain disruptions, economic volatility, and regulatory changes can impact retailers' operations and profitability. However, with these challenges come opportunities for innovation, differentiation, and customer engagement. Retailers that embrace change, leverage technology, and prioritize customer-centric strategies are best positioned to thrive in the evolving retail landscape.

Conclusion:
As we embark on this exploration of the retail industry, it's essential to recognize the pivotal role it plays in shaping our economy, culture, and daily lives. From its humble origins to its modern-day manifestations, retail continues to evolve and adapt to meet the ever-changing needs of consumers. By understanding the historical context, structural dynamics, and key trends shaping the industry, we can gain valuable insights into its present state and future trajectory. Whether you're a seasoned industry veteran or a newcomer to the field, the journey ahead promises to be one of discovery, innovation, and opportunity in the vibrant world of retail.

Chapter: Importance of Retail Sales in Business Success

Retail sales serve as the lifeblood of businesses across industries, playing a pivotal role in driving revenue, profitability, and growth. In this chapter, we'll explore the significance of retail sales in achieving business success and the various ways in which effective sales strategies contribute to organizational objectives.

Revenue Generation:
At its core, retail sales are instrumental in generating revenue for businesses by facilitating the exchange of goods and services for monetary compensation. Whether through brick-and-mortar storefronts, online platforms, or other distribution channels, retail sales represent a direct source of income that sustains operations, funds investments, and drives shareholder value. For businesses of all sizes, maximizing sales volume and optimizing pricing strategies are essential for achieving financial sustainability and long-term profitability.

Customer Acquisition and Retention:

Beyond mere transactions, retail sales serve as a gateway to acquiring and retaining customers—a fundamental driver of business success. By delivering exceptional shopping experiences, providing value-added services, and building trust and rapport with consumers, retailers can attract new customers and foster loyalty among existing ones. Repeat business and word-of-mouth referrals are invaluable assets in today's competitive marketplace, underscoring the importance of prioritizing customer satisfaction and relationship-building in retail sales.

Market Expansion and Brand Visibility:
Successful retail sales strategies not only drive revenue and customer loyalty but also contribute to market expansion and brand visibility. Through effective marketing, merchandising, and promotional efforts, retailers can increase brand awareness, differentiate themselves from competitors, and penetrate new markets. Whether through strategic partnerships, innovative product offerings, or experiential retail concepts, retailers have the opportunity to elevate their brand presence and create memorable impressions that resonate with consumers.

Data Insights and Decision-Making:
In an era of data-driven decision-making, retail sales provide valuable insights into consumer behavior, market trends, and operational performance. By leveraging data analytics, retailers can analyze sales metrics, track inventory levels, and identify opportunities for optimization and growth. From forecasting demand to personalizing marketing campaigns, data-driven insights empower retailers to make informed decisions that drive business success and enhance the overall customer experience.

Employee Engagement and Performance:

Retail sales also play a crucial role in fostering employee engagement, satisfaction, and performance. Sales associates and frontline staff serve as brand ambassadors, representing the face of the business and interacting directly with customers on a daily basis. By providing training, support, and incentives for sales staff, retailers can empower their teams to deliver exceptional service, achieve sales targets, and cultivate positive relationships with customers. A motivated and engaged workforce is essential for driving sales performance and enhancing the overall reputation and profitability of the business.

Conclusion:
In summary, retail sales are fundamental to achieving business success across multiple dimensions, including revenue generation, customer acquisition, market expansion, data-driven decision-making, and employee engagement. By recognizing the importance of retail sales and investing in effective sales strategies, businesses can position themselves for sustainable growth, competitive advantage, and long-term viability in today's dynamic marketplace. As we delve deeper into the intricacies of retail sales in the chapters ahead, we'll explore strategies and best practices for maximizing sales effectiveness and driving organizational success in the ever-evolving world of retail.

Chapter: Introducing the Retail Sales Book: Your Ultimate Guide to Excelling in Retail

Welcome to "Retail Sales Book: Your Ultimate Guide to Excelling in Retail," a comprehensive handbook designed to equip you with the knowledge, skills, and strategies needed to thrive in the dynamic world of retail sales. In this introductory chapter, we'll explore the purpose and scope of this book, as well as what you can expect to gain from its pages.

Purpose:
At its core, this book is a testament to the transformative power of retail sales—a discipline that combines art, science, and psychology to drive business success and enhance the customer experience. Whether you're a seasoned sales professional seeking to sharpen your skills or a newcomer eager to make your mark in the industry, this book is your roadmap to achieving excellence in retail sales. Through a blend of theoretical insights, practical techniques, and real-world examples, we aim to empower you with the tools and knowledge needed to succeed in today's competitive retail landscape.

Scope:
"Retail Sales Book" is a comprehensive guide that covers a wide range of topics essential to mastering the art of retail sales. From understanding consumer behavior and effective communication to leveraging data analytics and building customer relationships, each chapter is meticulously crafted to provide you with actionable insights and practical strategies for success. Whether you're interested in honing your selling techniques, optimizing your personal brand, or navigating industry trends, this book has something for everyone.

What to Expect:
As you journey through the pages of this book, you'll encounter a wealth of valuable information, including:

Insights into the psychology of selling and persuasion
Strategies for mastering product knowledge and effective communication
Techniques for delivering exceptional customer service and building customer loyalty
Best practices for leveraging data and analytics to drive sales performance
Guidance on developing your personal brand and advancing your career in retail sales
Each chapter is designed to build upon the concepts introduced in the previous ones, creating a comprehensive and cohesive learning experience that will empower you to excel in every aspect of retail sales.

Conclusion:

Whether you're a sales associate, store manager, or business owner, "Retail Sales Book" is your ultimate companion on the journey to retail success. By immersing yourself in the principles, strategies, and techniques outlined in this book, you'll gain the knowledge and confidence needed to excel in today's fast-paced retail environment. So, let's embark on this transformative journey together, as we unlock the secrets to mastering the art of retail sales and achieving unparalleled success in the exciting world of retail.

Chapter: Understanding the Retail Landscape

Welcome to the Retail Sales Book, your comprehensive guide to mastering the intricate landscape of retail sales. In this chapter, we embark on a journey to explore the multifaceted world of retail, gaining insights into its evolution, structure, and key trends that shape the industry's trajectory.

Evolution of Retail:
Retail is not merely an economic activity but a reflection of societal evolution and technological progress. From ancient marketplaces to modern-day digital storefronts, the retail landscape has undergone profound transformations over the centuries. We'll delve into the historical roots of retail, tracing its evolution from local bazaars and trading posts to the globalized, technologically-driven marketplace we know today. Understanding this historical context provides valuable insights into the forces shaping the current retail landscape and offers clues to its future direction.

Structure of the Retail Industry:
The retail industry is a vast and diverse ecosystem comprised of various players, formats, and channels. From traditional brick-and-mortar stores to online marketplaces, retailers operate in a myriad of formats catering to different consumer needs and preferences. We'll explore the different types of retail formats, from department stores and specialty shops to discount chains and e-commerce platforms. Understanding the structural dynamics of the retail industry is essential for navigating its complexities and identifying opportunities for growth and innovation.

Key Trends and Forces Shaping Retail:
The retail industry is constantly evolving, driven by shifting consumer behaviors, technological advancements, and global economic trends. We'll examine some of the key trends and forces shaping the retail landscape, including the rise of e-commerce, the growing importance of sustainability and ethical consumerism, and the impact of emerging technologies such as artificial intelligence and augmented reality. By staying abreast of these trends, retailers can anticipate changes in consumer preferences, adapt their strategies accordingly, and position themselves for success in a rapidly changing marketplace.

Challenges and Opportunities:
While the retail industry presents abundant opportunities for growth and innovation, it also presents its fair share of challenges. From increasing competition to changing regulatory landscapes, retailers must navigate a myriad of obstacles to stay ahead of the curve. We'll explore some of the challenges facing retailers today, such as supply chain disruptions, labor shortages, and the need to balance physical and digital retail experiences. Despite these challenges, there are also numerous opportunities for retailers to differentiate themselves, innovate, and create value for their customers. By embracing change and leveraging their strengths, retailers can overcome obstacles and thrive in an ever-evolving retail landscape.

Conclusion:

As we conclude this chapter, we're reminded that the retail landscape is a dynamic and ever-changing environment shaped by a myriad of factors. By understanding its historical roots, structural dynamics, and key trends, retailers can position themselves for success in an increasingly competitive marketplace. In the chapters ahead, we'll delve deeper into the principles, strategies, and best practices that underpin successful retail sales, equipping you with the knowledge and tools needed to excel in this exciting and dynamic industry.

Chapter: Evolution of Retail: From Brick-and-Mortar to Omnichannel

The evolution of retail is a fascinating journey that mirrors the progression of society, technology, and consumer behavior. In this chapter, we'll trace the transformation of retail from its humble beginnings as brick-and-mortar establishments to the modern-day omnichannel landscape that blurs the lines between physical and digital commerce.

Brick-and-Mortar Roots:
The story of retail begins with the earliest human civilizations, where traders and merchants bartered goods in bustling marketplaces. Over time, the concept of brick-and-mortar stores emerged, providing consumers with a physical location to browse, shop, and interact with products. From local shops and boutiques to department stores and shopping malls, brick-and-mortar retail became ingrained in the fabric of society, serving as vital hubs of economic activity and social exchange.

The Rise of E-Commerce:

The advent of the internet revolutionized the retail landscape, giving rise to e-commerce—a digital marketplace where consumers could shop from the comfort of their homes or on the go. Online retailers such as Amazon, eBay, and Alibaba disrupted traditional retail models, offering a vast selection of products, competitive pricing, and convenient delivery options. As consumers embraced the convenience and accessibility of online shopping, e-commerce emerged as a dominant force in the retail industry, reshaping consumer expectations and challenging brick-and-mortar retailers to adapt or risk obsolescence.

The Emergence of Omnichannel Retail:
Recognizing the changing retail landscape, forward-thinking retailers began to adopt an omnichannel approach—a seamless integration of online and offline channels to provide customers with a unified shopping experience. By leveraging technology such as mobile apps, social media, and data analytics, retailers could engage with consumers across multiple touchpoints, from browsing products online to making purchases in-store. Omnichannel retailing blurred the boundaries between physical and digital commerce, allowing retailers to meet customers wherever they are and deliver personalized, cohesive experiences that drive loyalty and satisfaction.

The Future of Retail:

As we look to the future, the retail landscape continues to evolve at a rapid pace, driven by technological innovation, shifting consumer preferences, and emerging market trends. From the rise of mobile commerce and voice-activated shopping to the potential impact of artificial intelligence and virtual reality, the possibilities for retail are limitless. However, amidst the excitement and uncertainty of the future, one thing remains clear—retailers must embrace innovation, adapt to changing consumer demands, and harness the power of omnichannel strategies to thrive in the digital age.

Conclusion:

The evolution of retail from brick-and-mortar to omnichannel represents a transformative shift in how consumers shop, engage with brands, and experience retail. By understanding the historical context, technological advancements, and consumer trends that have shaped the retail landscape, retailers can adapt their strategies, innovate their offerings, and create meaningful connections with customers in an increasingly competitive marketplace. As we continue our exploration of retail sales in the chapters ahead, we'll delve deeper into the principles, strategies, and best practices that underpin successful omnichannel retailing, equipping you with the knowledge and tools needed to excel in today's dynamic retail environment.

Chapter: Key Players in the Retail Industry

The retail industry is a vast and diverse ecosystem comprised of numerous players, each contributing to the complex tapestry of commerce in their own unique way. In this chapter, we'll explore some of the key players in the retail industry, from multinational corporations to small businesses, and examine their roles and contributions to the retail landscape.

Multinational Corporations:
At the top of the retail hierarchy are multinational corporations (MNCs) that dominate global markets with their vast networks, expansive product assortments, and economies of scale. Companies such as Walmart, Amazon, and Alibaba are household names synonymous with retail excellence, leveraging their size and resources to offer consumers unparalleled selection, value, and convenience. With operations spanning multiple countries and continents, MNCs wield significant influence over industry trends, supply chains, and consumer behavior.

Department Stores:

Department stores are a cornerstone of the retail industry, offering a wide range of merchandise across multiple categories under one roof. From apparel and cosmetics to home goods and electronics, department stores cater to diverse consumer preferences and shopping occasions. Iconic department store chains such as Macy's, Nordstrom, and Harrods are renowned for their upscale ambiance, curated product offerings, and exceptional customer service, attracting shoppers seeking luxury, variety, and personalized experiences.

Specialty Retailers:

Specialty retailers focus on specific product categories or niches, catering to distinct consumer segments with specialized merchandise and expertise. These retailers range from fashion boutiques and electronics stores to health and wellness outlets and pet supply shops. Examples include brands like Nike, Apple, Sephora, and PetSmart, which excel in their respective niches by offering unique products, innovative experiences, and expert guidance that resonate with their target audiences.

Discount Retailers:

In an era of budget-conscious consumers, discount retailers play a vital role in providing affordable, value-oriented shopping options. Discount retailers such as Walmart's subsidiary, Walmart Inc., and Target's subsidiary, Target Corporation, are known for their low prices, wide assortments, and convenient locations, attracting customers seeking everyday essentials at competitive prices. Other discount retailers, such as Dollar General and Aldi, specialize in offering limited assortments of deeply discounted merchandise, appealing to price-sensitive shoppers seeking bargains and savings.

E-Commerce Platforms:

The rise of e-commerce has revolutionized the retail landscape, enabling consumers to shop anytime, anywhere, with the click of a button. E-commerce platforms such as Amazon, eBay, and Alibaba have transformed the way people shop, offering unparalleled convenience, selection, and accessibility. These platforms leverage advanced technology, data analytics, and logistics capabilities to deliver seamless shopping experiences, personalized recommendations, and fast, reliable delivery to millions of customers worldwide.

Independent and Small Businesses:

Amidst the dominance of multinational corporations and e-commerce giants, independent and small businesses play a vital role in the retail ecosystem, bringing diversity, innovation, and local flavor to communities around the world. From family-owned boutiques and artisanal shops to pop-up markets and online storefronts, these businesses offer unique products, personalized service, and a sense of authenticity that resonates with consumers seeking one-of-a-kind experiences and supporting local economies.

Conclusion:

The retail industry is a dynamic and diverse ecosystem comprised of a multitude of players, each contributing to the vibrancy and vitality of commerce in their own unique way. Whether they're multinational corporations dominating global markets, department stores offering a wide range of merchandise, specialty retailers catering to niche audiences, discount retailers providing value-oriented options, e-commerce platforms revolutionizing the way people shop, or independent and small businesses bringing diversity and authenticity to communities, every player in the retail industry plays a vital role in shaping consumer experiences, driving economic growth, and defining the future of retail. As we continue our exploration of retail sales in the chapters ahead, we'll delve deeper into the strategies, challenges, and opportunities facing these key players, equipping you with the knowledge and insights needed to excel in the dynamic world of retail.

Chapter: Current Trends and Future Projections

In the fast-paced world of retail, staying ahead of trends and anticipating future developments is essential for success. In this chapter, we'll explore some of the current trends shaping the retail landscape and offer insights into future projections that will influence the industry in the years to come.

Current Trends:

E-Commerce Dominance:
The shift towards online shopping continues to accelerate, fueled by convenience, accessibility, and changing consumer preferences. E-commerce platforms such as Amazon, Alibaba, and Shopify have experienced exponential growth, capturing a larger share of retail sales and reshaping the traditional retail landscape. With the proliferation of mobile devices and advancements in technology, e-commerce is expected to remain a dominant force in retail, driving further innovation and competition in the digital space.

Omnichannel Integration:
Retailers are embracing omnichannel strategies to provide customers with seamless shopping experiences across multiple channels and touchpoints. Whether online, in-store, or through mobile devices, consumers expect a consistent and personalized experience at every stage of their shopping journey. Retailers that successfully integrate their physical and digital channels can enhance customer engagement, drive sales, and build loyalty in an increasingly competitive marketplace.

Personalization and Customization:

Consumers are demanding more personalized and tailored shopping experiences that cater to their individual preferences and needs. Retailers are leveraging data analytics, artificial intelligence, and machine learning algorithms to collect and analyze customer data, allowing them to deliver targeted marketing messages, personalized product recommendations, and customized promotions. By understanding customer behavior and preferences, retailers can create more meaningful connections with their audience and drive sales.

Sustainability and Ethical Consumerism:
Increasing awareness of environmental and social issues is driving a shift towards sustainability and ethical consumerism in retail. Consumers are increasingly seeking out eco-friendly products, ethically sourced goods, and socially responsible brands that align with their values. Retailers that prioritize sustainability initiatives, transparent supply chains, and corporate social responsibility are well-positioned to attract environmentally and socially conscious consumers and differentiate themselves in the market.

Future Projections:

Continued Growth of E-Commerce:
The e-commerce boom is expected to continue as consumers embrace online shopping as a preferred mode of retail. As technology evolves and consumer expectations evolve, e-commerce platforms will continue to innovate and expand their offerings, further disrupting traditional retail models and shaping the future of commerce.

Rise of Augmented Reality and Virtual Reality:

Technologies such as augmented reality (AR) and virtual reality (VR) have the potential to revolutionize the retail experience, allowing consumers to virtually try on clothing, visualize furniture in their homes, and explore products in immersive environments. As AR and VR technologies become more accessible and affordable, retailers will increasingly incorporate these tools into their marketing strategies, enhancing engagement and driving sales.

Expansion of Subscription Services:
Subscription-based models are gaining traction in retail, offering consumers convenience, variety, and value through recurring shipments of curated products or services. From meal kits and beauty boxes to clothing rentals and streaming services, subscription-based retail offers retailers a recurring revenue stream and provides consumers with a hassle-free shopping experience tailored to their preferences.
Continued Emphasis on Customer Experience:

In an increasingly competitive retail landscape, customer experience will remain a top priority for retailers seeking to differentiate themselves and drive loyalty. From personalized interactions and frictionless transactions to immersive in-store experiences and exceptional customer service, retailers that prioritize customer experience will gain a competitive edge and foster long-term relationships with their audience.

Conclusion:

As we look to the future of retail, one thing is certain: change is inevitable. By staying informed about current trends and future projections, retailers can adapt their strategies, innovate their offerings, and position themselves for success in an ever-evolving marketplace. Whether it's embracing e-commerce, integrating omnichannel experiences, prioritizing sustainability, or leveraging emerging technologies, retailers that stay ahead of the curve will be well-positioned to thrive in the dynamic world of retail. As we continue our exploration of retail sales in the chapters ahead, we'll delve deeper into the strategies, tactics, and best practices that will shape the future of retail and empower you to excel in this exciting and ever-changing industry.

Chapter: The Impact of Technology on Retail Sales

In today's rapidly evolving retail landscape, technology plays a pivotal role in shaping consumer behavior, driving sales, and transforming the way retailers engage with their audience. In this chapter, we'll explore the profound impact of technology on retail sales and examine how retailers are leveraging innovative tools and strategies to stay ahead of the curve.

Enhanced Customer Experience:
Technology has revolutionized the retail experience, enabling retailers to deliver personalized, seamless, and immersive experiences that delight customers at every touchpoint. From interactive displays and virtual try-on experiences to mobile apps and chatbots, retailers are leveraging technology to create engaging and memorable interactions that drive customer satisfaction and loyalty.

Data-Driven Insights:
One of the most significant benefits of technology in retail sales is the ability to capture, analyze, and leverage vast amounts of data to gain insights into consumer behavior, preferences, and trends. By harnessing data analytics, retailers can identify patterns, anticipate demand, and tailor their offerings to meet the evolving needs of their audience. From optimizing product assortments and pricing strategies to personalizing marketing campaigns and promotions, data-driven insights empower retailers to make informed decisions that drive sales and profitability.

Omnichannel Integration:

Technology has blurred the lines between physical and digital retail, giving rise to the omnichannel shopping experience—a seamless integration of online and offline channels that provides customers with a cohesive and consistent experience across multiple touchpoints. Retailers are leveraging technologies such as mobile apps, RFID tags, and beacon technology to connect with customers wherever they are, allowing them to browse, shop, and interact with brands across various channels in a frictionless manner.

Automation and Efficiency:

Advancements in automation and robotics have streamlined retail operations, reducing costs, improving efficiency, and enhancing the overall customer experience. From automated inventory management systems and self-checkout kiosks to robotic warehouse fulfillment centers and drone delivery services, retailers are leveraging automation technologies to optimize processes, reduce human error, and deliver products to customers faster and more efficiently than ever before.

Personalization and Customization:

Technology enables retailers to deliver personalized and customized experiences that resonate with individual customers on a one-to-one level. By leveraging technologies such as artificial intelligence, machine learning, and predictive analytics, retailers can analyze customer data in real-time, identify preferences, and deliver targeted recommendations and offers tailored to each individual. Personalization enhances the shopping experience, increases engagement, and drives sales by making customers feel understood and valued.

Augmented Reality and Virtual Reality:

Emerging technologies such as augmented reality (AR) and virtual reality (VR) are revolutionizing the way consumers shop, allowing them to visualize products in real-world environments and make more informed purchasing decisions. Retailers are leveraging AR and VR technologies to create immersive shopping experiences, such as virtual fitting rooms, interactive product demonstrations, and virtual showroom tours, that engage customers and drive sales both online and in-store.

Conclusion:

The impact of technology on retail sales cannot be overstated. From enhancing customer experiences and driving sales to streamlining operations and optimizing efficiency, technology has become an indispensable tool for retailers seeking to thrive in today's competitive marketplace. By embracing innovation, leveraging data-driven insights, and adopting emerging technologies, retailers can position themselves for success and deliver value to customers in new and exciting ways. As we continue our exploration of retail sales in the chapters ahead, we'll delve deeper into the strategies, tactics, and best practices for harnessing the power of technology to drive sales and achieve retail excellence.

Chapter: The Psychology of Selling

At its core, retail sales is as much about understanding human psychology as it is about moving products off shelves. In this chapter, we'll delve into the fascinating world of the psychology of selling, exploring the key principles, strategies, and techniques that underpin successful sales interactions.

Understanding Customer Behavior:
Central to the psychology of selling is understanding the behavior, motivations, and decision-making processes of customers. Consumer behavior is influenced by a myriad of factors, including social, cultural, psychological, and situational variables. By understanding these factors, retailers can tailor their sales approaches to resonate with their target audience and effectively influence purchasing decisions.

Building Rapport and Trust:
Building rapport and establishing trust are essential components of successful sales interactions. Customers are more likely to buy from salespeople they like, trust, and feel understood by. By demonstrating empathy, active listening, and genuine interest in customers' needs and preferences, salespeople can build rapport and establish a foundation of trust that forms the basis of a successful sales relationship.

Creating Emotional Connections:

Emotions play a powerful role in driving purchasing decisions. Retailers that can evoke positive emotions such as joy, excitement, and satisfaction in their customers are more likely to influence buying behavior and drive sales. By tapping into customers' emotions through compelling storytelling, immersive experiences, and sensory cues, retailers can create emotional connections that resonate on a deeper level and inspire loyalty and repeat business.

Leveraging Social Proof:

Social proof—the psychological phenomenon where people rely on the actions and opinions of others to guide their own behavior—is a powerful tool in the arsenal of salespeople. Testimonials, reviews, endorsements, and social media influencers can all serve as forms of social proof that validate the quality, popularity, and desirability of products or services. By leveraging social proof effectively, retailers can overcome objections, build credibility, and persuade customers to make purchasing decisions.

Harnessing the Power of Persuasion:

Persuasion is the art of influencing others' beliefs, attitudes, and behaviors to achieve desired outcomes. In retail sales, persuasion techniques such as scarcity, authority, reciprocity, and consistency can be employed to nudge customers towards making a purchase. By framing products or offers in a compelling way, highlighting their unique features or benefits, and presenting them in the context of customers' needs or desires, salespeople can increase the likelihood of closing a sale.

Overcoming Objections:

In the course of a sales interaction, customers may raise objections or concerns that need to be addressed before they feel comfortable making a purchase. Effective salespeople anticipate objections and are prepared with responses that alleviate customers' concerns and reinforce the value proposition of the product or service. By listening attentively, acknowledging objections, and offering solutions or alternatives, salespeople can overcome objections and move the sales process forward.

Conclusion:

The psychology of selling is a complex and nuanced field that draws on principles from psychology, sociology, and communication theory to understand and influence customer behavior. By mastering the principles, strategies, and techniques outlined in this chapter, salespeople can build rapport, establish trust, create emotional connections, leverage social proof, harness the power of persuasion, and overcome objections to drive sales and achieve retail excellence. As we continue our exploration of retail sales in the chapters ahead, we'll delve deeper into the practical application of these principles and provide actionable strategies for maximizing sales effectiveness in various retail contexts.

Chapter: Understanding Consumer Behavior

Consumer behavior lies at the heart of retail sales, shaping the decisions customers make when purchasing products or services. In this chapter, we'll explore the intricacies of consumer behavior, examining the factors that influence how and why individuals make buying decisions.

Psychological Factors:
Consumer behavior is heavily influenced by psychological factors that impact individuals' perceptions, attitudes, and motivations. These factors include:
Perception: Consumers interpret and make sense of information based on their perceptions, which are shaped by their sensory experiences, past experiences, and cultural background.
Motivation: Consumers are driven by various needs and desires, such as the need for food, shelter, safety, social belonging, esteem, and self-actualization. Understanding consumers' motivations can help retailers tailor their offerings to meet these needs and create value for their customers.

Attitudes and Beliefs: Consumers' attitudes and beliefs towards products, brands, and retailers influence their purchasing decisions. Positive attitudes and strong brand beliefs can lead to increased loyalty and repeat purchases, while negative attitudes can deter customers from engaging with a brand or making a purchase.

Social Influences:

Social factors play a significant role in shaping consumer behavior, as individuals are influenced by the attitudes, opinions, and behaviors of others in their social networks. These social influences include:

Reference Groups: Consumers often look to reference groups—such as family, friends, colleagues, and social media influencers—for guidance and validation when making purchasing decisions. Positive references from influential groups can reinforce consumers' perceptions of a product or brand and encourage them to make a purchase.

Social Norms: Consumers conform to social norms and cultural expectations when making buying decisions, seeking to fit in with societal standards and expectations. Retailers can leverage social norms by aligning their products and marketing messages with prevailing cultural trends and values.

Social Identity: Consumers' sense of identity and self-concept influences their purchasing decisions, as they seek products and brands that reflect their personality, values, and lifestyle. By understanding consumers' social identities, retailers can tailor their offerings and marketing strategies to resonate with their target audience and foster a sense of belonging and affinity.

Economic and Situational Factors:

Consumer behavior is also influenced by economic and situational factors that impact individuals' ability and willingness to make purchases. These factors include:

Income and Budget Constraints: Consumers' purchasing decisions are constrained by their income levels, budgetary constraints, and financial priorities. Retailers can appeal to different income segments by offering products and services at various price points and providing financing options or discounts to make purchases more affordable.

Time and Convenience: Consumers' purchasing decisions are influenced by considerations of time and convenience, as they seek to minimize effort and maximize utility in their shopping experiences. Retailers can enhance convenience by offering flexible payment options, fast and reliable shipping, and convenient store locations and hours of operation.

Situational Context: Consumers' buying decisions are influenced by situational factors such as the occasion, urgency, and context of the purchase. Retailers can capitalize on situational cues by offering limited-time promotions, seasonal discounts, and special offers that align with consumers' needs and preferences.

Conclusion:

Understanding consumer behavior is essential for retailers seeking to connect with their target audience, anticipate their needs, and influence their purchasing decisions. By examining the psychological, social, economic, and situational factors that shape consumer behavior, retailers can tailor their offerings, marketing messages, and sales strategies to resonate with their audience and drive sales. As we continue our exploration of retail sales in the chapters ahead, we'll delve deeper into the practical application of consumer behavior principles and provide actionable strategies for maximizing sales effectiveness in various retail contexts.

Chapter: Principles of Persuasion and Influence

In the realm of retail sales, mastering the principles of persuasion and influence is essential for driving customer engagement, closing deals, and achieving sales success. In this chapter, we'll explore six key principles of persuasion outlined by psychologist Robert Cialdini and examine how they can be applied to retail sales.

Reciprocity:
The principle of reciprocity states that people feel compelled to reciprocate when someone does something for them. In retail sales, offering customers something of value, whether it's a sample, a discount, or personalized assistance, can create a sense of obligation to reciprocate by making a purchase. By providing value upfront and building goodwill with customers, retailers can increase the likelihood of closing a sale and fostering long-term relationships.
Scarcity:

The principle of scarcity suggests that people are more motivated to take action when they perceive that a product or opportunity is limited or scarce. Retailers can leverage scarcity by highlighting limited-time offers, exclusive products, or low stock levels to create a sense of urgency and FOMO (fear of missing out) among customers. By emphasizing the scarcity of a product or promotion, retailers can encourage customers to act quickly and make a purchase before it's too late.

Authority:

The principle of authority asserts that people are more likely to comply with requests or recommendations from perceived authorities or experts in a particular domain. In retail sales, leveraging the expertise and credibility of sales associates, industry influencers, or third-party endorsements can enhance the perceived authority of a product or brand and increase its appeal to customers. By positioning themselves as trusted advisors and sources of expertise, retailers can build trust and credibility with customers, leading to increased sales and loyalty.

Consistency:

The principle of consistency suggests that people have a strong desire to align their actions with their beliefs and commitments. In retail sales, obtaining small commitments from customers, such as signing up for a newsletter, taking a product demo, or agreeing to a trial offer, can increase the likelihood of securing a larger commitment, such as making a purchase. By eliciting small commitments and reinforcing consistency throughout the sales process, retailers can nudge customers towards taking action and closing the deal.

Liking:

The principle of liking posits that people are more likely to say yes to those they know, like, and trust. In retail sales, building rapport, establishing common ground, and finding shared interests with customers can increase likability and influence purchasing decisions. By demonstrating empathy, active listening, and genuine interest in customers' needs and preferences, retailers can create positive interactions that foster trust, rapport, and ultimately, sales.

Social Proof:

The principle of social proof suggests that people are more likely to take action when they see others doing the same. In retail sales, leveraging social proof through testimonials, reviews, ratings, and user-generated content can validate the quality, popularity, and desirability of a product or brand. By showcasing positive feedback and endorsements from satisfied customers, retailers can build credibility, overcome objections, and persuade hesitant buyers to make a purchase.

Conclusion:

By understanding and applying the principles of persuasion and influence outlined in this chapter, retailers can enhance their sales effectiveness, drive customer engagement, and achieve their sales goals. Whether it's offering value upfront to trigger reciprocity, creating urgency through scarcity, leveraging authority and expertise, eliciting small commitments to reinforce consistency, building rapport and likability with customers, or showcasing social proof to validate their offerings, retailers can use these principles to ethically persuade and influence customers to make purchasing decisions. As we continue our exploration of retail sales in the chapters ahead, we'll delve deeper into the practical application of these principles and provide actionable strategies for maximizing sales effectiveness in various retail contexts.

Chapter: Building Trust and Rapport with Customers

In the dynamic world of retail sales, building trust and rapport with customers is essential for fostering positive relationships, driving loyalty, and ultimately, closing deals. In this chapter, we'll explore strategies and techniques for building trust and rapport with customers, laying the foundation for successful sales interactions.

Active Listening:
Effective communication begins with active listening—paying close attention to customers' words, tone, and body language to understand their needs, preferences, and concerns. By listening attentively and empathetically, sales associates can demonstrate genuine interest in customers' perspectives, build rapport, and establish a connection based on trust and understanding.
Ask Open-Ended Questions:

Encourage meaningful dialogue and engagement with customers by asking open-ended questions that invite them to share their thoughts, feelings, and experiences. Open-ended questions prompt customers to elaborate on their needs and preferences, providing valuable insights that sales associates can use to tailor their recommendations and solutions to meet customers' specific needs.

Empathy and Understanding:

Demonstrate empathy and understanding towards customers' concerns, challenges, and goals by acknowledging their feelings and validating their experiences. By showing empathy and compassion, sales associates can create a supportive and non-judgmental environment that fosters trust, openness, and honesty in the sales interaction.

Provide Value and Solutions:

Deliver value to customers by offering personalized recommendations, solutions, and insights that address their unique needs and preferences. By positioning themselves as trusted advisors and problem-solvers, sales associates can build credibility and demonstrate their commitment to helping customers find the best possible solution to their needs.

Transparency and Honesty:

Build trust with customers by being transparent and honest in all interactions, including pricing, product information, and policies. Transparency fosters confidence and reassurance in customers, demonstrating integrity and a commitment to ethical business practices that prioritize their best interests.

Follow Through and Follow Up:

Demonstrate reliability and accountability by following through on promises and commitments made to customers. Whether it's providing updates on order status, resolving issues promptly, or following up after a sale to ensure satisfaction, proactive communication and responsiveness build trust and confidence in customers' minds.

Personalize the Experience:

Tailor the sales experience to each customer's preferences, interests, and past interactions to create a personalized and memorable experience. By remembering details about customers' preferences, acknowledging their past purchases, and anticipating their needs, sales associates can demonstrate attentiveness and thoughtfulness that deepen the connection and build rapport.

Express Appreciation and Gratitude:
Show appreciation and gratitude towards customers for their business, loyalty, and support. Whether it's a simple thank you message, a handwritten note, or a special discount or offer, expressing gratitude fosters goodwill and strengthens the bond between sales associates and customers.

Conclusion:

Building trust and rapport with customers is a foundational element of successful retail sales. By actively listening, asking open-ended questions, demonstrating empathy, providing value and solutions, being transparent and honest, following through and following up, personalizing the experience, and expressing appreciation and gratitude, sales associates can create positive and meaningful interactions that build trust, loyalty, and long-term relationships with customers. As we continue our exploration of retail sales in the chapters ahead, we'll delve deeper into the practical application of these strategies and provide actionable tips for building trust and rapport with customers in various retail contexts.

Chapter: Overcoming Objections and Handling Rejections

In the world of retail sales, objections and rejections are inevitable obstacles that sales professionals must learn to navigate with skill and confidence. In this chapter, we'll explore effective strategies for overcoming objections and handling rejections gracefully, turning challenges into opportunities for building trust and closing deals.

Anticipate Common Objections:
Proactive preparation is key to overcoming objections successfully. By anticipating common objections based on product features, pricing, timing, or other factors, sales professionals can develop persuasive responses and preemptively address customers' concerns before they arise. Understanding customers' potential objections allows sales professionals to build credibility and demonstrate expertise in guiding them towards a positive purchasing decision.
Listen Attentively and Empathetically:

When faced with objections, it's essential to listen attentively and empathetically to customers' concerns. Rather than immediately jumping to rebuttals or counterarguments, take the time to fully understand the reasons behind the objection and validate customers' perspectives. Active listening demonstrates respect for customers' opinions and fosters a collaborative atmosphere where objections can be addressed constructively.

Clarify and Probe Deeper:
Once an objection has been raised, seek clarification and probe deeper to uncover the underlying motivations or issues driving the objection. Ask open-ended questions to encourage customers to elaborate on their concerns and provide additional context. By gaining a deeper understanding of customers' objections, sales professionals can tailor their responses more effectively and address the root cause of the objection.

Provide Value and Address Concerns:
In responding to objections, focus on providing value and addressing customers' concerns in a clear and compelling manner. Highlight the benefits and advantages of the product or service in relation to customers' needs and preferences, and offer relevant solutions or alternatives that alleviate their concerns. Demonstrating empathy and understanding while offering practical solutions builds trust and reassurance, increasing customers' confidence in making a purchase.

Handle Objections Professionally:

Maintain a professional and respectful demeanor when handling objections, even in challenging situations. Avoid becoming defensive or argumentative, and refrain from dismissing customers' objections outright. Instead, acknowledge customers' viewpoints with empathy and sincerity, and respond calmly and confidently with well-reasoned explanations or solutions. By handling objections with professionalism and grace, sales professionals can preserve the integrity of the sales interaction and maintain positive rapport with customers.

Seek Agreement and Confirm Understanding:

Once objections have been addressed, seek agreement and confirm understanding with customers to ensure that their concerns have been adequately addressed. Encourage customers to voice any remaining questions or reservations, and provide further clarification or reassurance as needed. Confirming understanding and agreement helps to reinforce customers' confidence in their decision-making process and paves the way for closing the sale on a positive note.

Learn from Rejections:

Inevitably, not every objection will be successfully overcome, and some customers may ultimately choose not to make a purchase. Instead of viewing rejections as failures, see them as valuable learning opportunities for growth and improvement. Reflect on the reasons behind the rejection, identify any areas for improvement in the sales approach or product offering, and use the experience to refine your skills and strategies for future interactions.

Conclusion:

Overcoming objections and handling rejections effectively requires a combination of preparation, empathy, professionalism, and resilience. By anticipating common objections, listening attentively, clarifying concerns, providing value, handling objections professionally, seeking agreement, and learning from rejections, sales professionals can navigate objections with confidence and turn challenges into opportunities for building trust and closing deals. As we continue our exploration of retail sales in the chapters ahead, we'll delve deeper into the practical application of these strategies and provide actionable tips for overcoming objections and handling rejections in various retail contexts.

Chapter: Mastering Product Knowledge

In the world of retail sales, product knowledge is a powerful tool that empowers sales professionals to engage customers effectively, address their needs, and drive sales. In this chapter, we'll explore the importance of mastering product knowledge and provide strategies for acquiring, retaining, and leveraging comprehensive knowledge about the products or services being sold.

Importance of Product Knowledge:

Product knowledge forms the foundation of successful sales interactions, enabling sales professionals to communicate effectively with customers, answer questions confidently, and provide personalized recommendations based on customers' needs and preferences. By possessing in-depth knowledge about the features, benefits, applications, and value propositions of the products or services they sell, sales professionals can build credibility, instill confidence in customers, and ultimately, close more sales.

Acquiring Product Knowledge:

Acquiring comprehensive product knowledge requires a proactive and ongoing effort to research, study, and familiarize oneself with the products or services being sold. Sales professionals can leverage various resources to enhance their product knowledge, including product manuals, training materials, online resources, manufacturer specifications, and hands-on experience with the products themselves. Additionally, seeking guidance from colleagues, attending product training sessions, and participating in product demonstrations can provide valuable insights and deepen understanding.

Understanding Features and Benefits:

Beyond simply memorizing product specifications, sales professionals should focus on understanding the features and benefits of the products or services from the perspective of the customer. Features refer to the specific attributes or functionalities of the product, while benefits highlight the value or advantages that those features offer to the customer. By articulating how the features translate into tangible benefits that address customers' needs or solve their problems, sales professionals can effectively communicate the value proposition of the product and persuade customers to make a purchase.

Relating Products to Customer Needs:

Effective sales professionals go beyond reciting product features and benefits to actively listening to customers' needs and preferences and relating the products or services to those specific needs. By asking probing questions, uncovering customers' pain points or challenges, and identifying opportunities to provide solutions or recommendations, sales professionals can demonstrate how the products or services meet customers' needs and add value to their lives. This customer-centric approach builds trust, fosters engagement, and increases the likelihood of closing a sale.

Staying Updated and Refreshing Knowledge:

Product knowledge is not static; it evolves over time with updates, enhancements, and new releases. Sales professionals must stay updated on changes and developments in the products or services they sell and refresh their knowledge regularly to maintain relevance and accuracy. Whether it's attending refresher training sessions, reading product updates and announcements, or actively seeking out information from suppliers or manufacturers, staying informed ensures that sales professionals are equipped to provide accurate and up-to-date information to customers.

Leveraging Product Knowledge in Sales Interactions:

During sales interactions, sales professionals can leverage their product knowledge strategically to engage customers, address objections, and close sales. By highlighting key features and benefits that align with customers' needs, providing relevant examples or case studies to illustrate product value, and offering comparisons with alternative solutions, sales professionals can tailor their messaging to resonate with customers and influence their purchasing decisions effectively.

Conclusion:

Mastering product knowledge is a fundamental skill for success in retail sales, enabling sales professionals to engage customers effectively, address their needs, and drive sales. By acquiring comprehensive product knowledge, understanding features and benefits from the perspective of the customer, relating products to customer needs, staying updated and refreshing knowledge regularly, and leveraging product knowledge strategically in sales interactions, sales professionals can build credibility, instill confidence in customers, and ultimately, achieve sales excellence. As we continue our exploration of retail sales in the chapters ahead, we'll delve deeper into the practical application of product knowledge and provide actionable tips for maximizing sales effectiveness in various retail contexts.

Chapter: Importance of Product Knowledge in Retail Sales

Product knowledge serves as the cornerstone of successful retail sales interactions, shaping the customer experience and influencing purchasing decisions. In this chapter, we'll explore the paramount importance of product knowledge in retail sales and how it impacts customer engagement, trust-building, and sales effectiveness.

Building Customer Confidence:
Comprehensive product knowledge instills confidence in customers by demonstrating expertise, credibility, and authority. When sales professionals possess in-depth knowledge about the products or services they sell, they can answer customer questions accurately, provide detailed information about features and benefits, and address concerns or objections with confidence. This confidence reassures customers that they are making informed purchasing decisions and builds trust in the retailer and its offerings.

Providing Personalized Recommendations:
Product knowledge enables sales professionals to provide personalized recommendations tailored to each customer's unique needs, preferences, and circumstances. By understanding the features, benefits, and applications of the products or services, sales professionals can assess customers' requirements and recommend solutions that best meet their needs. This personalized approach enhances the customer experience, increases satisfaction, and improves the likelihood of closing a sale.

Differentiating from Competitors:

In a competitive retail landscape, product knowledge serves as a key differentiator that sets retailers apart from their competitors. When sales professionals possess deep knowledge about the products or services they sell, they can articulate unique selling points, advantages, and value propositions that differentiate their offerings from alternatives in the market. This differentiation helps retailers stand out, capture customers' attention, and win their business over competitors who may lack expertise or depth of product knowledge.

Building Trust and Credibility:

Customers are more likely to trust and do business with retailers who demonstrate a thorough understanding of their products or services. When sales professionals exhibit expertise and proficiency in discussing product features, benefits, and applications, they build credibility with customers and establish themselves as trusted advisors. This trust forms the foundation of positive customer relationships, fosters loyalty, and increases the likelihood of repeat business and referrals.

Handling Objections Effectively:

Product knowledge equips sales professionals with the tools and information needed to address customer objections effectively. By understanding common objections and having prepared responses based on a deep understanding of the products or services, sales professionals can alleviate customers' concerns, overcome objections, and provide reassurance that leads to closing the sale. Handling objections with confidence and competence demonstrates professionalism and reinforces customers' confidence in their purchasing decisions.

Enhancing Sales Effectiveness:

Ultimately, product knowledge enhances sales effectiveness by empowering sales professionals to engage customers effectively, address their needs, and close deals successfully. When sales professionals possess comprehensive product knowledge, they can navigate sales interactions with confidence, tailor their recommendations to customers' preferences, and provide value-added solutions that drive sales and revenue growth for the retailer.

Conclusion:

Product knowledge is a critical asset for sales professionals in the retail industry, shaping the customer experience, building trust, and driving sales effectiveness. By investing in product knowledge development, retailers can equip their sales teams with the skills and expertise needed to engage customers effectively, differentiate from competitors, and achieve sales excellence. As we continue our exploration of retail sales in the chapters ahead, we'll delve deeper into strategies for acquiring, retaining, and leveraging product knowledge to maximize sales performance in various retail contexts.

Chapter: Strategies for Learning and Retaining Product Information

Acquiring and retaining comprehensive product knowledge is a continuous process that requires dedication, curiosity, and strategic learning techniques. In this chapter, we'll explore effective strategies for sales professionals to learn about products and services and retain that information for use in retail sales interactions.

Immersive Training Programs:
Immersive training programs provide sales professionals with hands-on experience and in-depth instruction on the products or services they will be selling. These programs may include product demonstrations, simulations, role-playing exercises, and interactive learning modules designed to engage participants and reinforce key concepts. By immersing themselves in the learning experience, sales professionals can develop a deeper understanding of the products or services and retain information more effectively.

Utilize Various Learning Resources:
Take advantage of a variety of learning resources to acquire and reinforce product knowledge. These resources may include product manuals, spec sheets, training videos, online courses, webinars, and manufacturer websites. By accessing a diverse range of resources, sales professionals can gain different perspectives and insights into the products or services they sell, enhancing their overall understanding and retention of key information.

Break Down Information into Digestible Chunks:

Breaking down product information into smaller, digestible chunks can make it easier to learn and retain. Instead of trying to memorize large amounts of information all at once, focus on mastering one aspect of the product or service at a time. Break down complex concepts into simpler components, and use mnemonic devices, visual aids, or diagrams to help organize and remember key information.

Engage in Active Learning Techniques:

Active learning techniques encourage active participation and engagement in the learning process, enhancing retention and understanding. Instead of passively consuming information, actively engage with the material by asking questions, participating in discussions, and applying concepts to real-world scenarios. Actively engaging with the material stimulates critical thinking, reinforces learning, and improves retention of product knowledge.

Teach Others:

Teaching others is an effective way to solidify your understanding of product information and reinforce your knowledge. Take on the role of a mentor or trainer and share your knowledge with colleagues or new hires. Teaching others forces you to articulate concepts clearly, answer questions, and provide explanations, which strengthens your own understanding and retention of the material.

Regular Review and Practice:

Regular review and practice are essential for retaining product information over time. Set aside dedicated time each week to review product features, benefits, and applications, and quiz yourself on key concepts to reinforce learning. Additionally, practice applying your product knowledge in simulated sales scenarios or role-playing exercises to hone your skills and build confidence in your ability to communicate effectively with customers.

Seek Feedback and Guidance:

Seek feedback and guidance from colleagues, mentors, or supervisors to identify areas for improvement and deepen your understanding of product information. Collaborate with teammates to share insights and best practices, and don't hesitate to ask for clarification or assistance when needed. By soliciting feedback and guidance, you can refine your product knowledge and enhance your sales effectiveness over time.

Conclusion:

Learning and retaining product information is a continuous journey that requires dedication, curiosity, and strategic learning techniques. By immersing yourself in immersive training programs, utilizing various learning resources, breaking down information into digestible chunks, engaging in active learning techniques, teaching others, regularly reviewing and practicing, and seeking feedback and guidance, you can acquire and retain comprehensive product knowledge that empowers you to excel in retail sales. As we continue our exploration of retail sales in the chapters ahead, we'll delve deeper into practical strategies for leveraging product knowledge to engage customers effectively and drive sales success.

Chapter: How to Tailor Product Knowledge to Different Customer Segments

In retail sales, effectively tailoring product knowledge to different customer segments is essential for engaging customers, addressing their unique needs, and maximizing sales opportunities. In this chapter, we'll explore strategies for customizing product knowledge to resonate with diverse customer segments and enhance the overall retail sales experience.

Understand Customer Segments:
The first step in tailoring product knowledge to different customer segments is to understand the characteristics, preferences, and needs of each segment. Conduct market research, analyze customer data, and segment your customer base based on factors such as demographics, psychographics, purchasing behavior, and preferences. By gaining insights into the distinct characteristics and preferences of each customer segment, you can tailor your product knowledge and sales approach to resonate with their specific needs and interests.
Identify Segment-Specific Needs and Preferences:

Once you've segmented your customer base, identify the unique needs, preferences, and pain points of each segment. Consider factors such as age, gender, lifestyle, income level, purchasing behavior, and product preferences to understand what matters most to each segment. For example, younger customers may prioritize convenience and technology features, while older customers may value reliability and durability. By identifying segment-specific needs and preferences, you can tailor your product knowledge to highlight the features and benefits that are most relevant and compelling to each segment.

Customize Messaging and Communication Style:
Tailor your messaging and communication style to resonate with the preferences and communication preferences of each customer segment. Use language, tone, and messaging that align with the values, interests, and communication styles of each segment. For example, younger customers may respond well to casual, conversational language and social media engagement, while older customers may prefer more formal, informative communication channels such as email or in-person interactions. By customizing your messaging and communication style, you can effectively engage each customer segment and convey product information in a way that resonates with their preferences.

Highlight Relevant Features and Benefits:
Focus on highlighting product features and benefits that are most relevant and compelling to each customer segment. Tailor your product knowledge to emphasize the aspects of the product that align with the needs, preferences, and priorities of each segment. For example, if you're selling electronics, emphasize the performance and technical specifications to tech-savvy customers, while highlighting ease of use and user-friendly features to less tech-savvy customers. By highlighting relevant features and benefits, you can demonstrate the value of the product in a way that resonates with each customer segment.

Provide Segment-Specific Examples and Use Cases:
Illustrate the value and applicability of the product to each customer segment by providing segment-specific examples and use cases. Tailor your product knowledge to showcase how the product can address the specific needs and challenges faced by each segment. For example, if you're selling kitchen appliances, provide examples of how the product can simplify meal preparation for busy families, enhance cooking capabilities for culinary enthusiasts, or save space for apartment dwellers. By providing segment-specific examples and use cases, you can demonstrate the relevance and utility of the product to each customer segment.

Offer Personalized Recommendations and Solutions:
Tailor your product knowledge to offer personalized recommendations and solutions that meet the unique needs and preferences of each customer segment. Leverage your understanding of each segment's preferences and priorities to recommend products or services that align with their specific requirements. For example, if you're selling skincare products, offer personalized recommendations based on each customer's skin type, concerns, and preferences. By offering personalized recommendations and solutions, you can demonstrate your expertise and add value to the customer experience, increasing the likelihood of closing the sale.

Conclusion:

Tailoring product knowledge to different customer segments is essential for engaging customers, addressing their unique needs, and maximizing sales opportunities in retail sales. By understanding the characteristics, preferences, and needs of each customer segment, customizing messaging and communication style, highlighting relevant features and benefits, providing segment-specific examples and use cases, and offering personalized recommendations and solutions, sales professionals can effectively engage diverse customer segments and drive sales success. As we continue our exploration of retail sales in the chapters ahead, we'll delve deeper into practical strategies for leveraging customer segmentation to optimize sales performance and enhance the overall customer experience.

Chapter: Leveraging Product Knowledge to Upsell and Cross-Sell

In retail sales, upselling and cross-selling are valuable strategies for increasing revenue and maximizing the value of each customer interaction. Leveraging product knowledge effectively is key to successfully implementing these strategies. In this chapter, we'll explore how sales professionals can leverage their product knowledge to upsell and cross-sell products or services to customers.

Understand Customer Needs and Preferences:
Before attempting to upsell or cross-sell, it's essential to understand the needs, preferences, and buying behavior of the customer. By engaging in active listening and asking probing questions, sales professionals can uncover opportunities to recommend additional products or services that align with the customer's needs and preferences. Understanding the customer's goals and motivations enables sales professionals to tailor their upselling and cross-selling efforts effectively.

Identify Complementary Products or Services:
Leverage your product knowledge to identify complementary products or services that enhance the value of the customer's purchase. Look for products or services that complement the original purchase and provide additional benefits or functionalities that meet the customer's needs. For example, if a customer is purchasing a camera, you could upsell accessories such as lenses, tripods, or camera bags, or cross-sell related products such as memory cards or photography books.

Highlight Value-Added Benefits:
When upselling or cross-selling, emphasize the value-added benefits of the additional products or services to the customer. Highlight how the complementary products or services enhance the original purchase and provide additional value or convenience. For example, if a customer is purchasing a laptop, you could highlight the benefits of purchasing an extended warranty for added peace of mind or a software subscription for enhanced functionality and security.

Demonstrate Product Expertise:
Demonstrate your product expertise and knowledge to build trust and credibility with the customer. Provide detailed information about the features, benefits, and applications of the additional products or services, and explain how they complement the customer's original purchase. By showcasing your expertise and demonstrating a deep understanding of the products or services, you can instill confidence in the customer and increase their willingness to consider upselling or cross-selling options.

Tailor Recommendations to Customer Preferences:
Tailor your upselling and cross-selling recommendations to align with the customer's preferences and interests. Consider factors such as the customer's previous purchase history, browsing behavior, and stated preferences to personalize your recommendations effectively. By offering relevant and targeted upselling and cross-selling suggestions, you can increase the likelihood of customer acceptance and satisfaction.

Anticipate Objections and Address Concerns:

Anticipate potential objections or concerns that customers may have about upselling or cross-selling and be prepared to address them effectively. Use your product knowledge to proactively address any concerns and provide reassurance to the customer. For example, if a customer expresses hesitancy about purchasing additional accessories, highlight the value and benefits of the accessories in enhancing their overall experience with the product.

Provide Incentives or Discounts:

Offer incentives or discounts to incentivize customers to consider upselling or cross-selling options. Provide special promotions, bundle discounts, or loyalty rewards to sweeten the deal and make the additional purchase more appealing to the customer. By providing incentives or discounts, you can encourage customers to explore upselling and cross-selling options and increase the likelihood of making an additional purchase.

Conclusion:

Leveraging product knowledge effectively is essential for successful upselling and cross-selling in retail sales. By understanding customer needs and preferences, identifying complementary products or services, highlighting value-added benefits, demonstrating product expertise, tailoring recommendations to customer preferences, anticipating objections, and providing incentives or discounts, sales professionals can effectively upsell and cross-sell products or services to customers, increasing revenue and enhancing the overall customer experience. As we continue our exploration of retail sales in the chapters ahead, we'll delve deeper into practical strategies for maximizing upselling and cross-selling opportunities and driving sales success.

Chapter: Effective Communication Skills

Effective communication is at the heart of successful retail sales interactions, enabling sales professionals to connect with customers, build rapport, and convey product information persuasively. In this chapter, we'll explore essential communication skills that are key to achieving sales excellence in the retail industry.

Active Listening:
Active listening is the foundation of effective communication in retail sales. It involves fully engaging with the customer, paying attention to their verbal and nonverbal cues, and demonstrating genuine interest in their needs and preferences. By listening attentively and empathetically, sales professionals can gain valuable insights into customers' requirements, identify opportunities for upselling or cross-selling, and build trust and rapport with the customer.
Clear and Concise Communication:

Clear and concise communication is essential for conveying product information effectively and avoiding misunderstandings. Sales professionals should articulate their messages clearly, using simple and straightforward language that is easy for customers to understand. Avoid jargon or technical terms that may confuse customers, and focus on communicating key points succinctly to ensure clarity and comprehension.

Tailoring Communication to Customer Preferences:
Recognize that different customers may have different communication preferences, and adapt your communication style accordingly. Some customers may prefer a more casual and conversational approach, while others may respond better to a more formal and professional demeanor. Pay attention to the customer's tone, body language, and communication style, and tailor your communication to align with their preferences for maximum impact.

Asking Probing Questions:
Asking probing questions is an effective way to gather information, uncover customer needs, and guide the sales conversation in the right direction. Sales professionals should ask open-ended questions that encourage customers to elaborate on their preferences, challenges, and goals. By probing deeper and actively engaging the customer in dialogue, sales professionals can gain a better understanding of their needs and tailor their recommendations accordingly.

Empathetic Communication:
Empathetic communication involves understanding and acknowledging the customer's perspective, feelings, and concerns. Sales professionals should demonstrate empathy by showing understanding, compassion, and sensitivity towards the customer's needs and emotions. Acknowledge any frustrations or challenges the customer may be experiencing, and offer reassurance and support to address their concerns effectively.

Confidence and Assertiveness:

Confidence and assertiveness are essential qualities that inspire trust and credibility in the eyes of the customer. Sales professionals should speak with confidence and conviction, demonstrating belief in the products or services they are selling. Be assertive in presenting recommendations and addressing objections, while also remaining respectful and considerate of the customer's preferences and decisions.

Active Engagement and Body Language:

Active engagement and positive body language are critical components of effective communication in retail sales. Maintain eye contact, smile, and use gestures and facial expressions to convey warmth and enthusiasm. Lean forward slightly to demonstrate attentiveness and engagement, and nod occasionally to signal understanding and agreement. By projecting confidence and enthusiasm through your body language, you can create a welcoming and engaging atmosphere that encourages open communication and trust.

Clarifying and Confirming Understanding:

Throughout the sales interaction, it's essential to clarify and confirm understanding to ensure that both parties are on the same page. Paraphrase the customer's questions or concerns to confirm your understanding, and provide clear and accurate responses to address them effectively. Encourage the customer to ask questions or seek clarification as needed, and confirm their understanding of the information provided before proceeding further.

Conclusion:

Effective communication skills are fundamental to success in retail sales, enabling sales professionals to connect with customers, convey product information persuasively, and build trust and rapport. By practicing active listening, communicating clearly and concisely, tailoring communication to customer preferences, asking probing questions, demonstrating empathy, projecting confidence and assertiveness, engaging actively with positive body language, and clarifying and confirming understanding, sales professionals can enhance the overall customer experience and achieve sales excellence. As we continue our exploration of retail sales in the chapters ahead, we'll delve deeper into practical strategies for mastering communication skills and maximizing sales effectiveness in various retail contexts.

Chapter: The Power of Effective Communication in Retail Sales

Effective communication lies at the heart of successful retail sales interactions, serving as a catalyst for building strong customer relationships, driving sales, and fostering loyalty. In this chapter, we'll explore the profound impact of effective communication on retail sales and the strategies for harnessing its power to achieve sales excellence.

Establishing Connection and Rapport:

Effective communication is instrumental in establishing a genuine connection and rapport with customers from the moment they step into the store or initiate contact. By greeting customers warmly, engaging in friendly conversation, and demonstrating genuine interest in their needs and preferences, sales professionals can create a welcoming atmosphere that puts customers at ease and sets the stage for a positive sales interaction. Establishing a personal connection fosters trust and rapport, making customers more receptive to the sales pitch and more likely to make a purchase.

Conveying Product Information Persuasively:

In retail sales, the ability to convey product information persuasively is crucial for influencing customers' purchasing decisions. Sales professionals should use clear and compelling language to highlight the features, benefits, and value propositions of the products or services they are selling. By articulating the unique selling points and advantages of the products in a way that resonates with the customer's needs and preferences, sales professionals can capture their interest and persuade them to make a purchase.

Building Trust and Credibility:

Effective communication builds trust and credibility with customers, positioning sales professionals as trusted advisors and experts in their field. By demonstrating expertise, professionalism, and integrity in their communication, sales professionals can instill confidence in customers and reassure them that their needs will be met. Trust is a cornerstone of successful sales relationships, and by fostering trust through effective communication, sales professionals can cultivate long-term customer loyalty and repeat business.

Overcoming Objections and Resolving Concerns:

In the course of a sales interaction, customers may raise objections or express concerns that need to be addressed effectively. Effective communication enables sales professionals to listen attentively to customers' objections, acknowledge their concerns, and respond with persuasive counterarguments or solutions. By demonstrating empathy, understanding, and responsiveness in their communication, sales professionals can overcome objections, alleviate concerns, and reassure customers, ultimately leading to a successful sale.

Creating Memorable Customer Experiences:

Exceptional communication has the power to create memorable customer experiences that leave a lasting impression and differentiate the retailer from its competitors. By delivering personalized and attentive service, actively engaging customers in meaningful conversation, and going above and beyond to meet their needs, sales professionals can create positive and memorable experiences that customers will remember long after the sale is complete. Memorable customer experiences build loyalty, generate positive word-of-mouth referrals, and contribute to the overall success of the retail business.

Enhancing Sales Effectiveness and Driving Revenue Growth:

Ultimately, effective communication is a catalyst for enhancing sales effectiveness and driving revenue growth in retail sales. By mastering communication skills, sales professionals can engage customers more effectively, convey product information persuasively, overcome objections, and create memorable customer experiences that lead to increased sales and customer satisfaction. The power of effective communication extends beyond individual sales transactions to impact the overall success and profitability of the retail business.

Conclusion:

Effective communication is a cornerstone of success in retail sales, enabling sales professionals to establish connections with customers, convey product information persuasively, build trust and credibility, overcome objections, create memorable customer experiences, and drive revenue growth. By harnessing the power of effective communication, sales professionals can achieve sales excellence, foster customer loyalty, and propel the retail business to new heights of success. As we continue our exploration of retail sales in the chapters ahead, we'll delve deeper into practical strategies for mastering communication skills and maximizing sales effectiveness in various retail contexts.

Chapter: Verbal and Nonverbal Communication Techniques

In retail sales, mastering both verbal and nonverbal communication techniques is essential for effectively engaging customers, conveying product information, and building rapport. In this chapter, we'll explore the importance of both verbal and nonverbal communication and provide practical techniques for leveraging them to enhance sales interactions.

Verbal Communication Techniques:
Verbal communication encompasses the spoken words and language used to convey information, persuade customers, and facilitate interactions. Here are some key verbal communication techniques for sales professionals:

Clear and Concise Language: Use clear and concise language to convey product information and recommendations effectively. Avoid jargon or technical terms that may confuse customers, and focus on communicating key points in a straightforward manner.
Active Listening: Actively listen to customers' questions, concerns, and preferences, and respond thoughtfully to demonstrate understanding. Paraphrase and repeat back key points to ensure clarity and show that you are engaged in the conversation.
Asking Open-Ended Questions: Ask open-ended questions that encourage customers to elaborate on their needs, preferences, and challenges. This allows you to gather valuable information and tailor your recommendations to meet their specific requirements.
Using Positive Language: Use positive language and phrasing to create a welcoming and supportive atmosphere. Frame recommendations and responses in a positive light to inspire confidence and enthusiasm in the customer.
Nonverbal Communication Techniques:
Nonverbal communication involves gestures, facial expressions, body language, and other nonverbal cues that convey meaning and emotions. Here are some key nonverbal communication techniques for sales professionals:

Eye Contact: Maintain appropriate eye contact with customers to demonstrate attentiveness and engagement. Avoid staring or looking away, as this can be perceived as disinterest or insincerity.

Facial Expressions: Use facial expressions to convey warmth, sincerity, and enthusiasm. Smile genuinely to create a positive and inviting atmosphere, and adjust your facial expressions to match the tone and content of the conversation.

Body Language: Pay attention to your body language and posture to convey confidence and professionalism. Stand or sit up straight, avoid crossing your arms or legs, and use open gestures to signal openness and receptivity.

Mirroring and Matching: Mirroring and matching the customer's nonverbal cues can help establish rapport and build a connection. subtly mimic the customer's gestures, posture, and tone of voice to create a sense of familiarity and mutual understanding.

Space and Proximity: Respect the customer's personal space and adjust your proximity accordingly. Maintain an appropriate distance that feels comfortable for the customer and allows for easy conversation without invading their personal space.

By mastering both verbal and nonverbal communication techniques, sales professionals can create a positive and engaging sales experience that resonates with customers and inspires confidence in the products or services being offered. As we continue our exploration of retail sales in the chapters ahead, we'll delve deeper into practical strategies for leveraging verbal and nonverbal communication to maximize sales effectiveness and customer satisfaction.

Chapter: Active Listening and Asking Powerful Questions

Active listening and asking powerful questions are foundational skills for effective communication in retail sales. By mastering these techniques, sales professionals can gain valuable insights into customer needs, preferences, and motivations, leading to more meaningful interactions and increased sales opportunities. In this chapter, we'll explore the importance of active listening and powerful questioning and provide practical strategies for incorporating them into sales interactions.

Active Listening:

Active listening involves fully engaging with the customer, focusing on what they are saying, and demonstrating genuine interest in their needs and concerns. Here are key elements of active listening:

Pay Attention: Give the customer your full attention by eliminating distractions and focusing on what they are saying. Avoid interrupting or thinking about your response while the customer is speaking.
Empathize: Put yourself in the customer's shoes and try to understand their perspective. Show empathy by acknowledging their feelings and validating their concerns.
Paraphrase and Summarize: Paraphrase the customer's statements and summarize key points to demonstrate understanding. This shows that you are actively engaged in the conversation and encourages the customer to elaborate further.
Ask Clarifying Questions: Ask clarifying questions to ensure that you have understood the customer's needs and preferences correctly. This helps prevent misunderstandings and ensures that you can provide relevant recommendations.
Asking Powerful Questions:
Powerful questions are thought-provoking, open-ended inquiries that encourage customers to reflect on their needs, preferences, and goals. Here are strategies for asking powerful questions:

Open-Ended Questions: Ask open-ended questions that require more than a simple "yes" or "no" answer. This encourages the customer to elaborate on their thoughts and provides valuable insights into their needs and preferences.
Probing Questions: Use probing questions to delve deeper into specific areas of interest or concern. Probe for details, examples, and explanations to gain a comprehensive understanding of the customer's requirements.

Hypothetical Questions: Pose hypothetical scenarios or "what if" questions to encourage the customer to consider different possibilities and options. This can help uncover hidden needs or preferences and stimulate creative thinking.

Reflective Questions: Ask reflective questions that prompt the customer to reflect on their past experiences or future aspirations. This can help uncover underlying motivations and desires that influence their purchasing decisions.

Solution-Focused Questions: Ask solution-focused questions that focus on identifying solutions or resolving challenges. Encourage the customer to envision a positive outcome and explore how your products or services can help them achieve their goals.

By incorporating active listening and powerful questioning into sales interactions, sales professionals can deepen their understanding of customer needs, uncover valuable insights, and build stronger relationships. These techniques enable sales professionals to provide more personalized recommendations and solutions that resonate with customers and ultimately lead to increased sales and customer satisfaction. As we continue our exploration of retail sales in the chapters ahead, we'll delve deeper into practical strategies for mastering active listening and asking powerful questions to maximize sales effectiveness and drive business success.

Chapter: Handling Difficult Customers with Grace and Professionalism

Encountering difficult customers is an inevitable aspect of retail sales, but how sales professionals respond to these situations can significantly impact the outcome and overall customer experience. In this chapter, we'll explore strategies for handling difficult customers with grace and professionalism, turning challenging interactions into opportunities to build trust and loyalty.

Maintain Calm and Composure:
When faced with a difficult customer, it's essential to remain calm and composed, regardless of the situation's intensity. Take a deep breath, center yourself, and approach the interaction with a positive and empathetic mindset. By maintaining your composure, you can diffuse tension and demonstrate professionalism, which is key to resolving the situation effectively.
Listen Empathetically:

Listen to the customer's concerns attentively and empathetically, allowing them to express their frustrations or grievances fully. Avoid interrupting or becoming defensive, and instead, show genuine interest in understanding their perspective. Reflect back their concerns to confirm understanding and validate their feelings, demonstrating empathy and building rapport.

Stay Solution-Focused:

Focus on finding a solution to the customer's problem rather than dwelling on the issue itself. Collaborate with the customer to identify their needs and explore possible resolutions together. Offer alternatives or compromises when appropriate, and strive to find a mutually beneficial outcome that satisfies the customer while aligning with company policies and guidelines.

Remain Professional and Respectful:

Maintain a professional demeanor and treat the customer with respect and courtesy, regardless of their behavior. Avoid taking things personally or responding emotionally to negative remarks or criticism. Instead, respond calmly and professionally, addressing the customer's concerns with dignity and integrity. By maintaining a respectful attitude, you can defuse hostility and maintain control of the situation.

Set Boundaries Firmly but Politely:

In some cases, it may be necessary to set boundaries with difficult customers to ensure a productive and respectful interaction. Assertively communicate company policies or limitations while remaining polite and courteous. Clearly explain what you can and cannot do to resolve the customer's issue, and offer alternative solutions or escalate the matter to a supervisor if necessary. Setting boundaries demonstrates assertiveness and professionalism while maintaining control of the situation.

Offer Appreciation and Follow-Up:

Once the issue has been resolved, express gratitude to the customer for their patience and understanding, regardless of the outcome. Thank them for bringing the issue to your attention and for giving you the opportunity to address it. Follow up with the customer after the interaction to ensure their satisfaction and reinforce your commitment to their needs. By offering appreciation and follow-up, you can leave a positive impression and turn a challenging interaction into an opportunity to build trust and loyalty.

Conclusion:

Handling difficult customers with grace and professionalism is a vital skill for sales professionals in the retail industry. By maintaining calm and composure, listening empathetically, staying solution-focused, remaining professional and respectful, setting boundaries firmly but politely, and offering appreciation and follow-up, sales professionals can effectively navigate challenging interactions and turn them into opportunities to build trust and loyalty with customers. As we continue our exploration of retail sales in the chapters ahead, we'll delve deeper into practical strategies for managing difficult situations and enhancing the overall customer experience.

Chapter: The Art of Selling Techniques

In retail sales, mastering the art of selling involves a combination of strategic techniques, interpersonal skills, and customer-centric approaches. In this chapter, we'll explore the key selling techniques that sales professionals can leverage to effectively engage customers, convey value, and drive sales.

Building Rapport:
Building rapport with customers is the foundation of successful selling. Establishing a genuine connection and rapport with customers creates a positive and trusting atmosphere that sets the stage for a successful sales interaction. Use friendly greetings, engage in small talk, and find common ground to build rapport and make customers feel comfortable and valued.

Understanding Customer Needs:
Effective selling begins with understanding and addressing customer needs. Take the time to listen actively to customers' concerns, preferences, and challenges. Ask probing questions to uncover their needs and motivations, and tailor your recommendations accordingly. By understanding customer needs, you can position your products or services as solutions that meet their specific requirements.

Highlighting Benefits, Not Features:

Focus on highlighting the benefits of your products or services rather than just listing their features. Help customers understand how your offerings can solve their problems, fulfill their desires, or improve their lives. Emphasize the value proposition and unique selling points of your products or services to demonstrate their relevance and appeal to customers.

Demonstrating Value:

Demonstrate the value of your products or services by showcasing their features in action. Use demonstrations, samples, or testimonials to illustrate how your offerings can benefit customers. Highlight success stories or case studies to provide real-life examples of how your products or services have helped others. By demonstrating value, you can increase customer confidence and willingness to make a purchase.

Overcoming Objections:

Address customer objections confidently and effectively to overcome resistance and move the sales process forward. Listen attentively to customer concerns and acknowledge their objections empathetically. Provide persuasive counterarguments or solutions to address their objections and alleviate any doubts or hesitations they may have. By addressing objections proactively, you can build trust and credibility with customers and increase the likelihood of closing the sale.

Closing the Sale:

Closing the sale is the culmination of the sales process and requires confidence, assertiveness, and finesse. Use closing techniques such as trial closes, assumptive closes, or urgency closes to prompt customers to make a purchasing decision. Ask for the sale directly and guide customers through the final steps of the transaction with clarity and professionalism. Be prepared to handle any last-minute objections or concerns and provide reassurance as needed.

Following Up:

Following up with customers after the sale is essential for building long-term relationships and fostering repeat business. Express gratitude for their purchase and inquire about their satisfaction with the product or service. Offer assistance or support as needed and provide additional value-added services, such as product tutorials or loyalty rewards. By following up with customers, you can reinforce their positive experience and encourage future purchases.

Conclusion:

Mastering the art of selling requires a combination of strategic techniques, interpersonal skills, and customer-centric approaches. By building rapport, understanding customer needs, highlighting benefits, demonstrating value, overcoming objections, closing the sale, and following up with customers, sales professionals can effectively engage customers, convey value, and drive sales. As we continue our exploration of retail sales in the chapters ahead, we'll delve deeper into practical strategies for mastering the art of selling and achieving sales excellence.

Chapter: The Sales Process: From Greeting to Closing

The sales process in retail encompasses a series of steps designed to guide customers through their purchasing journey, from the initial greeting to the closing of the sale. In this chapter, we'll break down each stage of the sales process and explore strategies for effectively navigating each step to drive sales success.

Greeting and Building Rapport:
The sales process begins with the initial greeting, where sales professionals have the opportunity to make a positive first impression. Greet customers warmly and authentically, using friendly body language and a welcoming tone of voice. Engage in small talk to build rapport and establish a connection with the customer. Take the time to listen attentively to the customer's responses and demonstrate genuine interest in their needs and preferences.
Needs Assessment:

Once rapport has been established, transition into the needs assessment phase by asking open-ended questions to uncover the customer's needs, preferences, and goals. Probe deeper to gain a comprehensive understanding of their requirements and motivations. Listen actively to the customer's responses and use empathetic listening skills to validate their concerns and demonstrate understanding. The needs assessment phase lays the groundwork for tailoring product recommendations to meet the customer's specific needs.

Product Presentation:

Based on the information gathered during the needs assessment phase, present products or services that align with the customer's needs and preferences. Highlight the features, benefits, and value propositions of the products or services in a clear and compelling manner. Use demonstrations, samples, or testimonials to illustrate how the offerings can address the customer's needs and solve their problems. Customize your presentation to resonate with the customer's interests and priorities, and be prepared to answer any questions or concerns they may have.

Overcoming Objections:

During the product presentation, anticipate and address any objections or concerns that the customer may raise. Listen empathetically to the customer's objections and acknowledge their concerns respectfully. Provide persuasive counterarguments or solutions to overcome their objections and alleviate any doubts or hesitations they may have. Use testimonials, case studies, or guarantees to reinforce the value and credibility of your offerings. By addressing objections effectively, you can build trust and credibility with the customer and move the sales process forward.

Closing the Sale:

The closing stage is the culmination of the sales process and involves guiding the customer through the final steps of making a purchasing decision. Use closing techniques such as trial closes, assumptive closes, or urgency closes to prompt the customer to make a decision. Ask for the sale directly and guide the customer through the transaction process with clarity and professionalism. Handle any last-minute objections or concerns with confidence and reassurance. Once the sale is closed, express gratitude to the customer for their purchase and provide assistance or support as needed.

Follow-Up and Relationship Building:

After the sale has been closed, follow up with the customer to ensure their satisfaction and reinforce the positive experience. Express gratitude for their purchase and inquire about their experience with the product or service. Offer additional support or assistance as needed and provide value-added services, such as product tutorials or loyalty rewards. Continue to nurture the customer relationship through ongoing communication and engagement, fostering loyalty and repeat business.

Conclusion:

The sales process in retail is a structured series of steps designed to guide customers through their purchasing journey, from the initial greeting to the closing of the sale. By effectively navigating each stage of the sales process, sales professionals can engage customers, address their needs, overcome objections, and ultimately drive sales success. As we continue our exploration of retail sales in the chapters ahead, we'll delve deeper into practical strategies for mastering each stage of the sales process and achieving sales excellence.

Chapter: Feature-Benefit Selling: Highlighting Product Value

Feature-benefit selling is a powerful technique used by sales professionals to effectively communicate the value of products or services to customers. In this chapter, we'll explore the concept of feature-benefit selling and provide strategies for highlighting product value to drive sales success.

Understanding Features and Benefits:
Features are the characteristics or attributes of a product or service, such as its specifications, functionalities, or design elements. Benefits, on the other hand, are the advantages or outcomes that customers derive from using the product or service. While features describe what the product is or does, benefits explain why it matters and how it can improve the customer's life or address their needs.
Aligning Features with Customer Needs:

To effectively highlight product value, sales professionals must align product features with customer needs and preferences. During the needs assessment phase of the sales process, identify the customer's pain points, challenges, or goals. Then, highlight product features that directly address these needs and provide tangible benefits to the customer. By emphasizing the relevance of product features to the customer's specific requirements, sales professionals can demonstrate the value and utility of the product.

Translating Features into Benefits:

Once product features have been identified, it's essential to translate them into meaningful benefits that resonate with the customer. For each feature, consider the corresponding benefit or outcome that it provides. Focus on how the product features can solve the customer's problems, fulfill their desires, or enhance their quality of life. Use language that emphasizes the positive impact of the product on the customer's well-being, productivity, or satisfaction. By articulating clear and compelling benefits, sales professionals can capture the customer's interest and motivate them to make a purchase.

Creating Value Propositions:

Craft value propositions that succinctly communicate the unique features and benefits of the product to the customer. A value proposition is a concise statement that outlines the value that the product offers to the customer and differentiates it from competitors. Focus on the most compelling features and benefits of the product, and tailor the value proposition to resonate with the customer's needs and priorities. Use persuasive language that highlights the product's advantages and positions it as the ideal solution for the customer's needs.

Providing Demonstrations and Examples:

Utilize demonstrations, examples, or case studies to illustrate how the product features translate into real-world benefits for the customer. Show the product in action and highlight its performance, reliability, or usability. Use testimonials or success stories from satisfied customers to provide social proof and reinforce the value of the product. By providing tangible evidence of the product's benefits, sales professionals can build credibility and confidence in the customer's mind.

Addressing Objections and Reinforcing Value:

During the sales interaction, anticipate and address any objections or concerns that the customer may have about the product. Listen attentively to the customer's objections and acknowledge their concerns respectfully. Provide persuasive counterarguments or solutions to overcome their objections and reinforce the value of the product. Emphasize the unique features and benefits that set the product apart from competitors and address the customer's specific needs. By addressing objections effectively and reinforcing the value of the product, sales professionals can build trust and confidence with the customer and increase the likelihood of closing the sale.

Conclusion:

Feature-benefit selling is a powerful technique for highlighting product value and driving sales success in retail. By aligning product features with customer needs, translating features into compelling benefits, creating value propositions, providing demonstrations and examples, and addressing objections effectively, sales professionals can effectively communicate the value of products or services to customers and motivate them to make a purchase. As we continue our exploration of retail sales in the chapters ahead, we'll delve deeper into practical strategies for mastering feature-benefit selling and achieving sales excellence.

Chapter: Creating Irresistible Offers and Promotions

Irresistible offers and promotions are powerful tools for attracting customers, driving sales, and fostering loyalty in the retail industry. In this chapter, we'll explore strategies for creating compelling offers and promotions that capture customers' attention, incentivize purchases, and generate excitement.

Understanding Customer Needs and Preferences:
Before creating offers and promotions, it's essential to understand your target audience's needs, preferences, and shopping behaviors. Conduct market research, analyze customer data, and gather feedback to identify trends, preferences, and pain points. Use this insight to tailor your offers and promotions to resonate with your target audience and address their specific needs and desires.
Offering Value-Added Benefits:

Create offers and promotions that provide tangible value-added benefits to customers. Consider offering discounts, incentives, or bonuses that make the offer irresistible and provide a clear advantage to the customer. Focus on benefits that are relevant and meaningful to your target audience, such as saving money, receiving free gifts, or gaining exclusive access to limited-time offers.

Leveraging Scarcity and Urgency:

Utilize scarcity and urgency tactics to create a sense of exclusivity and drive customer urgency. Offer limited-time promotions, flash sales, or exclusive deals that are available for a limited duration or in limited quantities. Use persuasive language and visuals to convey a sense of urgency and encourage customers to take immediate action to capitalize on the offer before it expires. Scarcity and urgency tactics can create a fear of missing out (FOMO) effect and motivate customers to make a purchase quickly.

Personalizing Offers and Recommendations:

Personalize offers and recommendations based on customer preferences, purchase history, and browsing behavior. Use data analytics and customer segmentation techniques to identify targeted groups of customers and tailor offers and promotions to their specific interests and preferences. Send personalized emails, offers, or recommendations to individual customers based on their unique needs and behaviors, creating a personalized shopping experience that enhances engagement and satisfaction.

Cross-Selling and Upselling Opportunities:

Identify cross-selling and upselling opportunities to maximize the value of each customer transaction. Offer complementary products or accessories that enhance the customer's purchase and provide additional value. Use suggestive selling techniques to recommend related products or upgrades that meet the customer's needs and preferences. By presenting relevant cross-selling and upselling opportunities, you can increase the average order value and drive incremental sales growth.

Promoting Through Multiple Channels:

Promote your offers and promotions through multiple channels to reach a broader audience and maximize visibility. Utilize digital channels such as email marketing, social media, and website banners to promote your offers to online audiences. Leverage traditional channels such as print advertisements, direct mail, and in-store signage to reach customers in physical locations. Consistency in messaging and branding across channels reinforces the offer's credibility and encourages customer engagement.

Measuring and Optimizing Performance:

Track and measure the performance of your offers and promotions to assess their effectiveness and identify areas for improvement. Monitor key metrics such as conversion rates, redemption rates, and return on investment (ROI) to evaluate the success of each promotion. Gather customer feedback and insights to understand how well the offer resonated with your target audience and identify opportunities for optimization. Use A/B testing and experimentation to refine your offers and strategies based on data-driven insights.

Conclusion:

Creating irresistible offers and promotions is essential for driving customer engagement, boosting sales, and building brand loyalty in the retail industry. By understanding customer needs and preferences, offering value-added benefits, leveraging scarcity and urgency, personalizing offers, identifying cross-selling and upselling opportunities, promoting through multiple channels, and measuring performance, retailers can create compelling promotions that capture customers' attention and drive business growth. As we continue our exploration of retail sales in the chapters ahead, we'll delve deeper into practical strategies for optimizing offers and promotions to achieve sales excellence.

Chapter: Creating Irresistible Offers and Promotions

Irresistible offers and promotions are powerful tools for attracting customers, driving sales, and fostering loyalty in the retail industry. In this chapter, we'll explore strategies for creating compelling offers and promotions that capture customers' attention, incentivize purchases, and generate excitement.

Understanding Customer Needs and Preferences:
Before creating offers and promotions, it's essential to understand your target audience's needs, preferences, and shopping behaviors. Conduct market research, analyze customer data, and gather feedback to identify trends, preferences, and pain points. Use this insight to tailor your offers and promotions to resonate with your target audience and address their specific needs and desires.

Offering Value-Added Benefits:
Create offers and promotions that provide tangible value-added benefits to customers. Consider offering discounts, incentives, or bonuses that make the offer irresistible and provide a clear advantage to the customer. Focus on benefits that are relevant and meaningful to your target audience, such as saving money, receiving free gifts, or gaining exclusive access to limited-time offers.

Leveraging Scarcity and Urgency:
Utilize scarcity and urgency tactics to create a sense of exclusivity and drive customer urgency. Offer limited-time promotions, flash sales, or exclusive deals that are available for a limited duration or in limited quantities. Use persuasive language and visuals to convey a sense of urgency and encourage customers to take immediate action to capitalize on the offer before it expires. Scarcity and urgency tactics can create a fear of missing out (FOMO) effect and motivate customers to make a purchase quickly.

Personalizing Offers and Recommendations:
Personalize offers and recommendations based on customer preferences, purchase history, and browsing behavior. Use data analytics and customer segmentation techniques to identify targeted groups of customers and tailor offers and promotions to their specific interests and preferences. Send personalized emails, offers, or recommendations to individual customers based on their unique needs and behaviors, creating a personalized shopping experience that enhances engagement and satisfaction.

Cross-Selling and Upselling Opportunities:

Identify cross-selling and upselling opportunities to maximize the value of each customer transaction. Offer complementary products or accessories that enhance the customer's purchase and provide additional value. Use suggestive selling techniques to recommend related products or upgrades that meet the customer's needs and preferences. By presenting relevant cross-selling and upselling opportunities, you can increase the average order value and drive incremental sales growth.

Promoting Through Multiple Channels:
Promote your offers and promotions through multiple channels to reach a broader audience and maximize visibility. Utilize digital channels such as email marketing, social media, and website banners to promote your offers to online audiences. Leverage traditional channels such as print advertisements, direct mail, and in-store signage to reach customers in physical locations. Consistency in messaging and branding across channels reinforces the offer's credibility and encourages customer engagement.

Measuring and Optimizing Performance:
Track and measure the performance of your offers and promotions to assess their effectiveness and identify areas for improvement. Monitor key metrics such as conversion rates, redemption rates, and return on investment (ROI) to evaluate the success of each promotion. Gather customer feedback and insights to understand how well the offer resonated with your target audience and identify opportunities for optimization. Use A/B testing and experimentation to refine your offers and strategies based on data-driven insights.

Conclusion:

Creating irresistible offers and promotions is essential for driving customer engagement, boosting sales, and building brand loyalty in the retail industry. By understanding customer needs and preferences, offering value-added benefits, leveraging scarcity and urgency, personalizing offers, identifying cross-selling and upselling opportunities, promoting through multiple channels, and measuring performance, retailers can create compelling promotions that capture customers' attention and drive business growth. As we continue our exploration of retail sales in the chapters ahead, we'll delve deeper into practical strategies for optimizing offers and promotions to achieve sales excellence.

Chapter: Techniques for Closing Sales and Securing Customer Loyalty

In the dynamic world of retail sales, mastering the art of closing deals and fostering customer loyalty is paramount. It's not just about making a sale; it's about creating lasting relationships that keep customers coming back for more. In this chapter, we'll explore some effective techniques for closing sales and securing customer loyalty that will help you thrive in the competitive retail landscape.

1. Active Listening:

The foundation of any successful sales interaction lies in active listening. Pay close attention to your customers' needs, preferences, and concerns. By truly understanding what they're looking for, you can tailor your approach to meet their specific requirements. Empathize with them and show genuine interest in solving their problems or fulfilling their desires.

2. Build Rapport:

Establishing a rapport with your customers is crucial for building trust and loyalty. Smile, make eye contact, and engage in friendly conversation to create a comfortable and welcoming environment. Remember details about your customers, such as their names, previous purchases, or personal preferences, and use this information to personalize their shopping experience.

3. Highlight Benefits:

Rather than focusing solely on the features of your products, emphasize the benefits they offer to the customer. How will this product improve their life or solve a problem they're facing? Paint a vivid picture of the positive outcomes they can expect, and how it aligns with their needs and desires.

4. Overcome Objections:

It's natural for customers to have objections or concerns before making a purchase. Instead of dismissing these objections, address them head-on with empathy and understanding. Provide relevant information or offer alternative solutions that alleviate their concerns and reassure them of the value they'll receive.

5. Create a Sense of Urgency:

Utilize scarcity and urgency techniques to motivate customers to make a decision. Highlight limited-time offers, exclusive deals, or low stock levels to create a sense of FOMO (fear of missing out). However, ensure that these tactics are genuine and transparent to maintain trust with your customers.

6. Trial Closes:

Throughout the sales process, use trial closes to gauge the customer's level of interest and readiness to make a purchase. Ask questions like, "Would you prefer this color or that one?" or "Are you leaning towards this product over others?" These subtle prompts can help guide the conversation towards a successful close.

7. Provide Exceptional Service:

Deliver exceptional service before, during, and after the sale to leave a lasting impression on your customers. Offer assistance, answer questions, and resolve any issues promptly and efficiently. Going above and beyond their expectations will not only secure the sale but also cultivate loyalty and encourage repeat business.

8. Follow-Up:

After the sale, don't forget to follow up with your customers to show appreciation for their business and ensure their satisfaction. Send personalized thank-you notes, request feedback on their experience, or offer post-purchase support and assistance. Building a relationship doesn't end after the sale — it's an ongoing process that requires continuous effort and attention.

By implementing these techniques into your sales strategy, you can effectively close more deals and foster long-term relationships with your customers. Remember, successful retail sales isn't just about transactions; it's about creating memorable experiences that keep customers coming back time and time again.

Chapter: Providing Exceptional Customer Service

In the ever-evolving landscape of retail, exceptional customer service stands as the cornerstone of success. It's the difference between a one-time transaction and a lifelong relationship. This chapter delves into the art of providing unparalleled customer service that leaves a lasting impression and keeps patrons coming back for more.

1. Empathy and Understanding:

At the heart of exceptional customer service lies empathy. Put yourself in the customer's shoes, understand their needs, concerns, and emotions. Whether they're seeking assistance or expressing dissatisfaction, approach each interaction with empathy and a genuine desire to help.

2. Active Listening:

Effective communication begins with active listening. Pay close attention to what your customers are saying, both verbally and non-verbally. By understanding their needs and preferences, you can offer tailored solutions that address their specific requirements.

3. Personalization:

Treat each customer as an individual with unique preferences and expectations. Personalize their shopping experience by remembering details about their previous purchases, preferences, and even personal milestones. Whether it's addressing them by name or recommending products based on their past interactions, personalization creates a sense of connection and fosters loyalty.

4. Timely and Efficient Assistance:

In today's fast-paced world, customers value prompt and efficient service. Be readily available to assist them, whether it's answering questions, providing product recommendations, or resolving issues. Minimize wait times and streamline processes to ensure a seamless and enjoyable shopping experience.

5. Anticipate Needs:

Go above and beyond to anticipate your customers' needs before they even express them. Offer proactive assistance, suggest complementary products, or provide relevant information to enhance their shopping experience. By anticipating their needs, you demonstrate your commitment to customer satisfaction and exceed their expectations.

6. Resolve Issues Gracefully:

Mistakes and issues are inevitable, but it's how you handle them that sets you apart. Respond to customer complaints or concerns promptly and gracefully. Apologize sincerely, take ownership of the situation, and work towards finding a satisfactory resolution. Turning a negative experience into a positive one not only retains the customer but also showcases your commitment to customer service excellence.

7. Educate and Inform:

Empower your customers with knowledge and information about your products or services. Educate them on features, benefits, and usage tips to help them make informed purchasing decisions. By acting as a trusted advisor rather than just a salesperson, you build credibility and earn their trust.

8. Follow-Up and Feedback:

After the sale, continue to nurture the relationship by following up with your customers. Express gratitude for their patronage and inquire about their satisfaction with their purchase. Encourage feedback and actively listen to their suggestions or concerns. Utilize this feedback to continually improve your products and services and strengthen customer relationships.

Exceptional customer service isn't just a goal—it's a commitment to prioritizing the needs and satisfaction of your customers above all else. By embodying empathy, active listening, personalization, and a dedication to continuous improvement, you can create memorable experiences that foster loyalty and set your retail business apart from the competition.

Chapter: Understanding the Importance of Customer Service in Retail

In the dynamic world of retail, where competition is fierce and consumer expectations are constantly evolving, exceptional customer service is not just a nice-to-have—it's a fundamental aspect of success. This chapter explores the significance of customer service in retail and why it should be a top priority for businesses of all sizes.

1. Building Customer Relationships:

Customer service serves as the foundation for building strong, long-lasting relationships with your clientele. When customers feel valued, heard, and supported, they are more likely to return to your store and become loyal patrons. Positive interactions with knowledgeable and attentive staff can leave a lasting impression and differentiate your brand from competitors.

2. Enhancing Customer Satisfaction:

Satisfied customers are the lifeblood of any retail business. By providing exceptional service that exceeds expectations, you can enhance customer satisfaction and loyalty. Whether it's offering personalized recommendations, resolving issues promptly, or going the extra mile to ensure a seamless shopping experience, every interaction contributes to overall satisfaction.

3. Differentiation in a Competitive Landscape:

In today's overcrowded marketplace, where consumers have endless options at their fingertips, standing out from the competition is essential. Exceptional customer service can be a powerful differentiator that sets your brand apart. When faced with similar products or prices, customers are more likely to choose the retailer that offers superior service and a memorable shopping experience.

4. Driving Repeat Business:

The key to sustainable success in retail lies in driving repeat business. Loyal customers not only return to make additional purchases but also become brand advocates who recommend your store to others. By consistently delivering exceptional service that exceeds expectations, you can cultivate a loyal customer base that drives revenue and sustains your business over the long term.

5. Increasing Customer Lifetime Value:

Customer service excellence has a direct impact on customer lifetime value (CLV). When customers have positive experiences and feel valued by your brand, they are more likely to increase their spending over time. By nurturing these relationships and providing ongoing support, you can maximize CLV and maximize the lifetime value of each customer to your business.

6. Mitigating Negative Word-of-Mouth:

In today's interconnected world, one negative customer experience can quickly snowball into a PR nightmare. Poor customer service can damage your brand's reputation and deter potential customers from patronizing your business. On the other hand, exceptional service not only mitigates negative word-of-mouth but also generates positive buzz and word-of-mouth referrals that attract new customers.

7. Adapting to Changing Consumer Expectations:

As consumer expectations continue to evolve, so too must your approach to customer service. Today's consumers demand convenience, personalization, and seamless omnichannel experiences. By staying attuned to these changing expectations and leveraging technology to enhance service delivery, you can future-proof your retail business and stay ahead of the curve.

8. Fostering a Culture of Excellence:

Exceptional customer service begins from within. By fostering a culture of excellence and empowerment among your employees, you can ensure that every interaction with customers reflects your brand values and commitment to service. Invest in training, provide support and recognition, and empower your staff to make decisions that prioritize the customer experience.

In summary, customer service is not just a department—it's a mindset that should permeate every aspect of your retail operation. By understanding the importance of customer service and prioritizing it as a strategic imperative, you can differentiate your brand, drive customer loyalty, and position your business for sustained success in the competitive retail landscape.

Chapter: Strategies for Delivering Outstanding Customer Experiences

In the fiercely competitive world of retail, delivering outstanding customer experiences isn't just a goal—it's a necessity. This chapter delves into key strategies that retailers can implement to ensure every interaction leaves a lasting positive impression on their customers.

1. Know Your Customers:

Understanding your customers' needs, preferences, and pain points is crucial for delivering exceptional experiences. Invest in gathering data and insights through customer surveys, purchase histories, and social listening. Use this information to personalize interactions and tailor your offerings to meet their specific requirements.

2. Train and Empower Your Team:

Your frontline employees are the face of your brand and play a pivotal role in shaping customer experiences. Provide comprehensive training that equips them with the knowledge, skills, and tools needed to deliver exceptional service. Empower them to make decisions autonomously and encourage a customer-centric mindset that prioritizes satisfaction above all else.

3. Streamline the Customer Journey:

Analyze and optimize every touchpoint along the customer journey to minimize friction and enhance convenience. From browsing and purchasing to post-sale support, ensure that each step is intuitive, seamless, and hassle-free. Leverage technology such as mobile apps, self-service kiosks, and chatbots to provide omnichannel experiences that cater to customers' preferences.

4. Foster Emotional Connections:

Emotions play a significant role in shaping customer perceptions and loyalty. Aim to create emotional connections that resonate with your customers on a deeper level. Whether it's through personalized communication, storytelling, or surprise and delight moments, evoke positive emotions that leave a lasting impression and foster strong brand affinity.

5. Anticipate and Exceed Expectations:

Go above and beyond to anticipate and exceed your customers' expectations at every opportunity. Surprise them with unexpected gestures, personalized recommendations, or proactive assistance. By consistently delivering more than they anticipate, you can delight customers and differentiate your brand from competitors.

6. Solicit and Act on Feedback:

Regularly solicit feedback from your customers through surveys, reviews, and social media channels. Actively listen to their suggestions, concerns, and preferences, and use this feedback to inform your strategy and improve the customer experience. Demonstrate your commitment to continuous improvement by implementing changes based on customer input.

7. Leverage Technology Wisely:

Technology can be a powerful enabler of exceptional customer experiences when used strategically. Implement tools and systems that enhance convenience, personalization, and efficiency, such as AI-powered chatbots, personalized recommendations engines, and seamless checkout processes. However, ensure that technology complements rather than detracts from the human touch and emotional connection.

8. Cultivate a Culture of Service Excellence:

Customer experience isn't just the responsibility of a single department—it's everyone's job. Cultivate a culture of service excellence throughout your organization by aligning values, recognizing and rewarding exceptional service, and fostering a customer-centric mindset at all levels. Encourage collaboration and teamwork to ensure that every employee plays a role in delivering outstanding experiences.

In conclusion, delivering outstanding customer experiences requires a holistic approach that encompasses understanding your customers, empowering your team, optimizing processes, and leveraging technology wisely. By implementing these strategies and prioritizing the customer at every touchpoint, retailers can differentiate their brand, drive loyalty, and position themselves for sustained success in today's competitive retail landscape.

Chapter: Handling Customer Complaints and Turning Them into Opportunities

In the world of retail, customer complaints are inevitable. However, how you handle these complaints can make all the difference between losing a customer and turning a negative experience into a positive one. This chapter explores effective strategies for handling customer complaints and leveraging them as opportunities to strengthen relationships and build loyalty.

1. Listen Actively and Empathize:

When a customer comes to you with a complaint, the first step is to listen actively and empathize with their concerns. Let them express their frustrations without interruption and show genuine understanding of their perspective. Empathy goes a long way in diffusing tension and demonstrating your commitment to resolving the issue.

2. Apologize Sincerely:

Offer a sincere apology for any inconvenience or dissatisfaction experienced by the customer. Regardless of whether the issue was within your control, expressing regret and taking ownership of the situation helps to validate the customer's feelings and begins the process of rebuilding trust.

3. Resolve the Issue Promptly:

Take swift action to address the customer's complaint and resolve the issue to their satisfaction. Whether it requires a refund, replacement, or additional assistance, prioritize finding a solution that meets the customer's needs. Keep the lines of communication open and provide regular updates on the progress of resolving the issue.

4. Go Above and Beyond:

In addition to addressing the immediate concern, consider going above and beyond to exceed the customer's expectations. Offer a small token of appreciation, such as a discount on their next purchase or a handwritten apology note. These gestures demonstrate your commitment to customer satisfaction and can turn a negative experience into a positive one.

5. Learn from Feedback:

View customer complaints as valuable feedback that can help you identify areas for improvement in your products, services, or processes. Analyze patterns and trends in complaints to pinpoint underlying issues and take proactive measures to prevent similar incidents in the future. By learning from feedback, you can continuously enhance the customer experience and mitigate future complaints.

6. Empower Your Team:

Empower your frontline staff with the authority and resources needed to address customer complaints effectively. Provide comprehensive training on conflict resolution, problem-solving, and customer service skills to equip them to handle complaints with confidence and professionalism. Encourage a culture of accountability and initiative, where employees feel empowered to take ownership of customer issues and find creative solutions.

7. Communicate Proactively:

Keep the customer informed throughout the resolution process to manage expectations and maintain transparency. Provide realistic timelines for resolving the issue and update the customer regularly on any progress or setbacks. Effective communication helps to reassure the customer that their concerns are being taken seriously and reinforces their trust in your brand.

8. Follow Up and Follow Through:

After the complaint has been resolved, follow up with the customer to ensure their satisfaction and inquire if there's anything else you can do to assist them. Demonstrate your commitment to their continued satisfaction by following through on any promises made during the resolution process. This final step reinforces your dedication to customer service excellence and leaves a positive lasting impression.

In conclusion, handling customer complaints effectively requires active listening, sincere apologies, swift resolution, and a commitment to learning and improvement. By viewing complaints as opportunities to strengthen relationships and build loyalty, retailers can turn dissatisfied customers into loyal advocates who appreciate the responsiveness and dedication to their satisfaction.

Chapter: Building Long-Term Relationships with Customers

In the competitive landscape of retail, fostering long-term relationships with customers is essential for sustained success. This chapter explores strategies for building strong connections, earning trust, and cultivating loyalty that extends beyond individual transactions.

1. Prioritize Customer Satisfaction:

At the core of building long-term relationships is a relentless focus on customer satisfaction. Every interaction, from the initial engagement to post-sale support, should be geared towards exceeding expectations and leaving a positive impression. Prioritize responsiveness, attentiveness, and personalized service to demonstrate your commitment to customer satisfaction.

2. Invest in Personalization:

Personalization is key to forging deeper connections with customers. Leverage data and insights to tailor the shopping experience to individual preferences, interests, and purchase history. Whether it's personalized recommendations, exclusive offers, or targeted communication, personalized experiences make customers feel valued and understood.

3. Communicate Consistently:

Maintain regular communication with your customers to stay top-of-mind and reinforce your relationship. Utilize email marketing, social media, and other channels to share relevant content, promotions, and updates. Keep the conversation two-way by soliciting feedback, responding promptly to inquiries, and engaging with customers on a personal level.

4. Offer Value Beyond Transactions:

Go beyond simply selling products and offer value-added services that enhance the customer experience. Whether it's educational resources, loyalty programs, or personalized styling advice, provide solutions that address your customers' needs and enrich their lives. By positioning your brand as a trusted advisor and partner, you can deepen customer loyalty and drive repeat business.

5. Create Memorable Experiences:

Memorable experiences leave a lasting impression and strengthen emotional connections with customers. Look for opportunities to surprise and delight them with unexpected gestures, personalized touches, or special events. Whether it's a handwritten thank-you note, a birthday discount, or an exclusive VIP event, these moments create positive associations and reinforce loyalty.

6. Anticipate and Adapt to Needs:

Stay attuned to evolving customer needs, preferences, and trends, and adapt your offerings accordingly. Anticipate future needs and proactively introduce new products, services, or features that align with your customers' evolving lifestyles and preferences. By demonstrating that you understand and anticipate their needs, you can position your brand as a trusted partner for the long term.

7. Build Trust and Transparency:

Trust is the foundation of any successful relationship. Be transparent in your communication, pricing, and policies to build trust and credibility with your customers. Honor commitments, resolve issues promptly, and prioritize honesty and integrity in all interactions. Trust is earned over time through consistent actions and demonstrates your commitment to building long-term relationships.

8. Solicit and Act on Feedback:

Regularly seek feedback from your customers to understand their experience, preferences, and areas for improvement. Actively listen to their suggestions, concerns, and feedback, and use this insight to inform your strategy and enhance the customer experience. By demonstrating that you value their input and are committed to continuous improvement, you reinforce your commitment to their satisfaction and loyalty.

In conclusion, building long-term relationships with customers requires a holistic approach that prioritizes satisfaction, personalization, communication, and trust. By consistently delivering exceptional experiences, offering value beyond transactions, and adapting to evolving needs, retailers can cultivate loyalty that extends far beyond individual purchases and drives sustainable growth and success.

Chapter: Harnessing the Power of Data and Analytics

In today's digital age, data has emerged as a powerful tool for retailers seeking to understand their customers, optimize operations, and drive growth. This chapter explores how retailers can harness the power of data and analytics to gain actionable insights and stay ahead in a competitive market.

1. Collecting Comprehensive Data:

The first step in leveraging data effectively is to collect comprehensive information about your customers, products, and operations. Utilize a variety of sources, including point-of-sale systems, online transactions, customer surveys, and website analytics, to gather data that provides a holistic view of your business.

2. Analyzing Customer Behavior:

By analyzing customer behavior data, retailers can gain valuable insights into their preferences, shopping habits, and purchasing patterns. Identify trends, segment customers based on demographics or buying behavior, and use predictive analytics to anticipate future needs and tailor marketing strategies accordingly.

3. Optimizing Inventory Management:

Data analytics can help retailers optimize inventory management by predicting demand, identifying slow-moving or obsolete stock, and optimizing replenishment cycles. By maintaining the right balance of stock levels, retailers can minimize stockouts, reduce carrying costs, and improve overall profitability.

4. Personalizing the Shopping Experience:

Personalization is key to engaging and retaining customers in a competitive market. Leverage customer data to personalize the shopping experience, whether through targeted product recommendations, customized promotions, or personalized messaging. By delivering relevant and timely content, retailers can enhance customer satisfaction and drive sales.

5. Enhancing Marketing Effectiveness:

Data-driven marketing allows retailers to target their marketing efforts more effectively and maximize ROI. Analyze customer data to identify high-value segments, optimize marketing channels, and tailor messaging to resonate with specific audiences. By delivering more relevant and personalized marketing campaigns, retailers can increase engagement and conversion rates.

6. Improving Operational Efficiency:

Data analytics can also be used to improve operational efficiency and streamline processes across the retail value chain. Identify inefficiencies, optimize staffing levels, and optimize store layouts based on foot traffic patterns. By leveraging data to make data-driven decisions, retailers can reduce costs, increase productivity, and enhance the overall customer experience.

7. Predictive Analytics and Forecasting:

Predictive analytics enables retailers to forecast future trends and make informed decisions about inventory management, pricing strategies, and marketing campaigns. By analyzing historical data and external factors, such as economic indicators or seasonal trends, retailers can anticipate demand fluctuations and adjust their strategies accordingly to stay ahead of the curve.

8. Ensuring Data Security and Compliance:

As retailers collect and analyze increasing amounts of customer data, it's essential to prioritize data security and compliance with privacy regulations. Implement robust security measures to protect sensitive data, and ensure compliance with regulations such as GDPR or CCPA. By safeguarding customer data and earning their trust, retailers can mitigate risk and build stronger customer relationships.

In conclusion, data and analytics offer retailers unprecedented opportunities to gain insights, optimize operations, and drive growth. By leveraging data effectively across all aspects of the business, retailers can gain a competitive edge, enhance the customer experience, and position themselves for long-term success in a rapidly evolving market.

Chapter: Introduction to Retail Analytics

In the digital age, the retail landscape is evolving at an unprecedented pace, driven by technological advancements and changing consumer behaviors. Amidst this transformation, retailers are increasingly turning to analytics to gain deeper insights into their operations, customers, and market trends. This chapter serves as an introduction to retail analytics, exploring its definition, significance, and key applications in the modern retail environment.

Defining Retail Analytics:

Retail analytics involves the collection, analysis, and interpretation of data to inform decision-making and drive business growth within the retail sector. It encompasses a wide range of data sources, including sales transactions, customer interactions, inventory levels, and market trends. By leveraging advanced analytical techniques and technologies, retailers can extract actionable insights from this data to optimize operations, enhance the customer experience, and drive profitability.

Significance of Retail Analytics:

In an increasingly competitive market, where margins are often slim and consumer expectations are high, retail analytics plays a pivotal role in helping retailers gain a competitive edge. By harnessing the power of data, retailers can make informed decisions that are grounded in evidence rather than intuition. Whether it's optimizing pricing strategies, identifying emerging trends, or personalizing the shopping experience, retail analytics enables retailers to stay agile, responsive, and ahead of the curve.

Key Applications of Retail Analytics:

Retail analytics offers a myriad of applications across various aspects of the retail value chain. Some key applications include:

Customer Segmentation and Targeting: Analyzing customer data to segment customers based on demographics, purchasing behavior, or preferences, and tailoring marketing strategies to target specific segments effectively.
Inventory Management: Utilizing predictive analytics to forecast demand, optimize inventory levels, and minimize stockouts or excess inventory.
Price Optimization: Analyzing pricing data, competitor pricing, and market trends to optimize pricing strategies and maximize profitability.
Visual Merchandising: Analyzing customer traffic patterns and engagement metrics to optimize store layouts, product placements, and visual merchandising strategies.
Marketing Effectiveness: Measuring the effectiveness of marketing campaigns, channels, and messaging through attribution analysis and ROI measurement.
Supply Chain Optimization: Analyzing supply chain data to identify bottlenecks, optimize logistics, and improve overall efficiency and cost-effectiveness.
Challenges and Considerations:

While the potential benefits of retail analytics are immense, implementing an effective analytics strategy also comes with its challenges. Retailers must navigate issues such as data quality, privacy concerns, technology integration, and organizational readiness. Moreover, the rapidly evolving nature of the retail landscape means that retailers must continuously adapt and innovate to stay ahead of the curve.

Conclusion:

In conclusion, retail analytics represents a powerful tool for retailers seeking to navigate the complexities of the modern retail landscape. By harnessing the power of data and analytics, retailers can gain deeper insights, make smarter decisions, and drive business growth in an increasingly competitive market. As retail analytics continues to evolve, its significance as a strategic imperative for retailers is only set to grow.

Chapter: Using Data to Understand Customer Preferences and Behavior

In the dynamic world of retail, understanding customer preferences and behavior is paramount to success. This chapter delves into the role of data in gaining insights into customer preferences and behavior, and how retailers can leverage this information to enhance the customer experience and drive business growth.

1. Data Collection and Integration:

The foundation of understanding customer preferences and behavior lies in collecting and integrating data from various sources. This includes transactional data, online interactions, social media engagement, demographic information, and more. By aggregating and analyzing these diverse data sets, retailers can gain a comprehensive understanding of their customers' preferences, behaviors, and motivations.

2. Segmentation and Profiling:

Once data is collected, retailers can segment their customer base into distinct groups based on common characteristics, such as demographics, purchasing behavior, or psychographic traits. By creating customer profiles or personas, retailers can tailor their marketing efforts, product offerings, and customer experiences to resonate with specific segments effectively.

3. Predictive Analytics:

Predictive analytics involves using historical data and statistical algorithms to forecast future trends and behaviors. Retailers can leverage predictive analytics to anticipate customer preferences, predict buying patterns, and identify opportunities for cross-selling or upselling. By proactively addressing customer needs and preferences, retailers can enhance the customer experience and drive sales.

4. Personalization and Customization:

Personalization is key to engaging customers and building lasting relationships. By leveraging data insights, retailers can personalize the shopping experience at every touchpoint, from product recommendations and promotional offers to email marketing and website content. Customizing the experience based on individual preferences and behaviors enhances relevance and increases the likelihood of conversion.

5. Journey Mapping and Optimization:

Customer journey mapping involves analyzing the various touchpoints and interactions that customers have with a brand throughout their purchasing journey. By mapping the customer journey and identifying pain points or areas for improvement, retailers can optimize the customer experience and remove friction from the buying process. This leads to higher satisfaction, increased loyalty, and improved retention rates.

6. Feedback Analysis:

Customer feedback is a valuable source of insights into preferences, satisfaction levels, and areas for improvement. By analyzing feedback from sources such as surveys, reviews, and social media, retailers can gain a deeper understanding of customer sentiment and identify opportunities for enhancement. Actively listening to customer feedback and taking action demonstrates a commitment to customer-centricity and continuous improvement.

7. Real-Time Insights:

In today's fast-paced retail environment, real-time insights are essential for staying agile and responsive to customer needs. Advanced analytics tools enable retailers to monitor customer behavior in real-time, identify trends as they emerge, and make data-driven decisions on the fly. By leveraging real-time insights, retailers can capitalize on opportunities, mitigate risks, and optimize the customer experience in the moment.

8. Ethical Considerations:

While data analytics offers immense potential for understanding customer preferences and behavior, retailers must also consider ethical considerations surrounding data privacy and security. It's essential to handle customer data responsibly, ensuring compliance with regulations such as GDPR or CCPA and maintaining transparency and trust with customers regarding data usage and protection.

In conclusion, data analytics provides retailers with a powerful tool for understanding customer preferences and behavior in unprecedented detail. By leveraging data insights to personalize the shopping experience, optimize operations, and drive innovation, retailers can build stronger relationships with customers, differentiate themselves in the market, and achieve sustainable growth in the long term.

Chapter: Implementing Data-Driven Strategies for Sales Optimization

In the fast-paced world of retail, the ability to make informed decisions based on data is crucial for driving sales and staying competitive. This chapter explores how retailers can harness the power of data-driven strategies to optimize sales performance and achieve sustainable growth.

1. Data Collection and Integration:

The first step in implementing data-driven strategies for sales optimization is to collect and integrate data from various sources. This includes transactional data, customer demographics, inventory levels, marketing campaigns, and more. By aggregating and centralizing this data, retailers can gain a comprehensive view of their sales performance and identify areas for improvement.

2. Sales Forecasting:

Data analytics enables retailers to forecast sales accurately, taking into account historical trends, seasonal variations, and external factors such as economic conditions or market trends. By leveraging predictive analytics algorithms, retailers can anticipate future demand, optimize inventory levels, and allocate resources more effectively to meet customer needs.

3. Customer Segmentation and Targeting:

Segmenting customers based on demographic, geographic, or behavioral characteristics allows retailers to tailor their sales strategies to specific customer segments effectively. By analyzing customer data, retailers can identify high-value segments, personalize marketing messages, and offer targeted promotions or product recommendations that resonate with individual preferences.

4. Pricing Optimization:

Data analytics enables retailers to optimize pricing strategies based on factors such as competitor pricing, demand elasticity, and customer willingness to pay. By analyzing pricing data and customer response, retailers can identify optimal price points, implement dynamic pricing strategies, and maximize profitability without sacrificing competitiveness.

5. Product Assortment Optimization:

Analyzing sales data and customer preferences allows retailers to optimize their product assortment to better meet customer demand. By identifying best-selling products, slow-moving items, and emerging trends, retailers can adjust their product mix, introduce new offerings, and optimize shelf space to maximize sales and minimize inventory costs.

6. Promotion Effectiveness:

Data analytics helps retailers measure the effectiveness of promotional campaigns and marketing initiatives. By analyzing sales data before, during, and after promotions, retailers can assess the impact on sales, customer acquisition, and profitability. This allows retailers to refine their promotional strategies, allocate resources more effectively, and maximize return on investment.

7. Sales Performance Analytics:

Monitoring sales performance metrics such as conversion rates, average transaction value, and sales per square foot provides retailers with valuable insights into the effectiveness of their sales strategies. By tracking key performance indicators (KPIs) in real-time and comparing against benchmarks or targets, retailers can identify areas for improvement, coach sales teams, and optimize sales processes to drive better results.

8. Continuous Improvement:

Implementing data-driven strategies for sales optimization is an ongoing process that requires continuous monitoring, analysis, and adaptation. By establishing a culture of data-driven decision-making, retailers can foster a mindset of continuous improvement and innovation. Regularly review performance metrics, solicit feedback from customers and employees, and iterate on strategies to stay agile and responsive to changing market dynamics.

In conclusion, leveraging data-driven strategies for sales optimization enables retailers to make smarter decisions, drive revenue growth, and gain a competitive edge in the retail landscape. By harnessing the power of data analytics to forecast sales, segment customers, optimize pricing and promotions, and monitor performance, retailers can unlock new opportunities for success and achieve sustainable growth in an increasingly dynamic and competitive market.

Chapter: Leveraging Analytics to Forecast Trends and Improve Decision-Making

In the ever-evolving landscape of retail, staying ahead of trends and making informed decisions is essential for success. This chapter explores how retailers can leverage analytics to forecast trends and enhance decision-making processes, enabling them to adapt quickly to changing market dynamics and gain a competitive edge.

1. Understanding Market Dynamics:

Analytics provides retailers with valuable insights into market dynamics, including consumer preferences, emerging trends, and competitive landscapes. By analyzing data from various sources, such as sales transactions, social media, and industry reports, retailers can identify patterns and trends that shape market behavior and anticipate future developments.

2. Predictive Analytics:

Predictive analytics enables retailers to forecast future trends and outcomes based on historical data and statistical models. By leveraging advanced algorithms, retailers can identify patterns, correlations, and causal relationships that drive market trends and make predictions with a high degree of accuracy. This allows retailers to anticipate changes in consumer behavior, demand fluctuations, and competitive movements, enabling them to proactively adjust their strategies and capitalize on emerging opportunities.

3. Demand Forecasting:

Demand forecasting is a critical aspect of retail planning, enabling retailers to optimize inventory levels, minimize stockouts, and maximize sales. By analyzing historical sales data, market trends, and external factors, retailers can predict future demand for products and services with precision. This allows retailers to align supply with demand, reduce excess inventory costs, and ensure optimal product availability to meet customer needs.

4. Trend Analysis:

Analyzing trends allows retailers to identify shifts in consumer preferences, purchasing behavior, and market dynamics. By monitoring key metrics and indicators, such as sales performance, product popularity, and social media mentions, retailers can track trends as they emerge and gain insights into their potential impact on the market. This enables retailers to adapt their product offerings, marketing strategies, and operations to capitalize on emerging trends and maintain relevance with consumers.

5. Competitive Intelligence:

Analytics provides retailers with valuable insights into competitors' strategies, performance, and market positioning. By analyzing data on competitors' pricing, promotions, product assortments, and customer feedback, retailers can identify strengths, weaknesses, and opportunities for differentiation. This allows retailers to benchmark their performance against competitors, identify areas for improvement, and develop strategies to outperform competitors in the market.

6. Scenario Planning:

Scenario planning involves evaluating multiple future scenarios based on different assumptions and variables to assess potential outcomes and mitigate risks. By using analytics to model different scenarios and simulate potential outcomes, retailers can identify potential challenges, opportunities, and uncertainties that may impact their business. This enables retailers to develop contingency plans, allocate resources more effectively, and make informed decisions that position them for success in any scenario.

7. Real-Time Monitoring and Alerts:

Real-time monitoring enables retailers to track key metrics and indicators in real-time and receive alerts about significant changes or anomalies. By leveraging analytics dashboards and automated alerts, retailers can stay informed about market developments, customer trends, and competitive movements as they happen. This enables retailers to react quickly to changes in the market and make timely decisions that drive business performance.

8. Data-Driven Decision-Making:

Ultimately, the goal of leveraging analytics is to empower retailers to make data-driven decisions that drive business success. By combining data, analytics, and domain expertise, retailers can make informed decisions that are grounded in evidence and aligned with strategic objectives. This enables retailers to optimize performance, mitigate risks, and capitalize on opportunities in an increasingly dynamic and competitive market.

In conclusion, leveraging analytics to forecast trends and improve decision-making enables retailers to adapt quickly to changing market dynamics, capitalize on emerging opportunities, and gain a competitive edge. By harnessing the power of predictive analytics, trend analysis, competitive intelligence, and scenario planning, retailers can make informed decisions that drive business growth and ensure long-term success in the retail landscape.

Chapter: Developing Your Personal Brand as a Retail Sales Professional

In the competitive world of retail sales, building a strong personal brand can set you apart from the crowd, establish credibility, and unlock new opportunities for career growth. This chapter explores strategies for developing your personal brand as a retail sales professional, enabling you to showcase your expertise, build meaningful connections, and achieve success in your career.

1. Define Your Unique Value Proposition:

Start by defining your unique value proposition—what sets you apart from other sales professionals? Identify your strengths, skills, and areas of expertise that make you valuable to employers and customers alike. Whether it's exceptional product knowledge, excellent communication skills, or a passion for customer service, articulate what makes you stand out in the competitive retail landscape.

2. Establish a Professional Online Presence:

In today's digital age, your online presence plays a crucial role in shaping your personal brand. Create professional profiles on platforms such as LinkedIn, showcasing your experience, skills, and achievements. Share relevant content, participate in industry discussions, and engage with peers and potential employers to build your online reputation as a knowledgeable and credible sales professional.

3. Showcase Your Expertise Through Content:

Demonstrate your expertise and thought leadership by creating and sharing valuable content related to retail sales. This could include blog posts, articles, videos, or social media posts offering insights, tips, and advice on topics relevant to your audience. By sharing your knowledge and insights, you position yourself as a trusted authority in your field and attract opportunities for collaboration and recognition.

4. Cultivate Relationships and Networks:

Networking is essential for building your personal brand and expanding your professional opportunities. Attend industry events, conferences, and meetups to connect with fellow professionals, industry influencers, and potential employers. Actively engage in conversations, seek out mentorship opportunities, and nurture relationships with peers and industry leaders to expand your network and unlock new opportunities.

5. Provide Exceptional Customer Service:

Your personal brand is intrinsically linked to the level of service you provide to your customers. Strive to deliver exceptional customer experiences at every opportunity, going above and beyond to exceed expectations and build lasting relationships. By consistently providing outstanding service, you earn the trust and loyalty of your customers, enhancing your reputation as a reliable and trustworthy sales professional.

6. Seek Feedback and Continuous Improvement:

Seek feedback from customers, colleagues, and mentors to gain insights into areas for improvement and development. Actively listen to feedback, both positive and constructive, and use it to refine your skills, enhance your performance, and strengthen your personal brand. Embrace a growth mindset and commit to continuous learning and improvement throughout your career.

7. Be Authentic and Consistent:

Authenticity is key to building a strong personal brand. Stay true to yourself and your values, and let your unique personality shine through in your interactions with customers and colleagues. Consistently demonstrate professionalism, integrity, and reliability in everything you do, both online and offline. By being genuine and consistent, you build trust and credibility with your audience, strengthening your personal brand in the process.

8. Showcase Your Successes and Achievements:

Don't be shy about showcasing your successes and achievements as a retail sales professional. Highlight your accomplishments, such as exceeding sales targets, winning awards, or receiving positive feedback from customers. Whether it's updating your LinkedIn profile, sharing success stories on social media, or including achievements in your resume, celebrate your wins and use them to reinforce your personal brand as a high-performing sales professional.

In conclusion, developing your personal brand as a retail sales professional requires a strategic approach, authenticity, and consistency. By defining your unique value proposition, establishing a professional online presence, showcasing your expertise, and delivering exceptional customer service, you can build a strong personal brand that opens doors to new opportunities and propels your career forward in the competitive world of retail sales.

Chapter: Understanding Personal Branding and Its Relevance in Retail Sales

In the dynamic realm of retail sales, personal branding is not just a buzzword—it's a strategic imperative. This chapter explores the concept of personal branding and its profound relevance in the context of retail sales professionals, elucidating how it can shape perception, drive success, and foster meaningful connections with customers and colleagues.

What is Personal Branding?

Personal branding is the intentional process of shaping and managing the public perception of oneself to differentiate and establish a unique identity in the minds of others. It involves defining your values, strengths, expertise, and unique attributes, and communicating them consistently across various channels to build credibility, trust, and recognition.

The Relevance of Personal Branding in Retail Sales

In the competitive landscape of retail sales, where products and services are often commoditized, personal branding serves as a powerful differentiator. Here's why it's particularly relevant:

1. Building Trust and Credibility:

A strong personal brand instills trust and credibility in the minds of customers. When customers perceive you as knowledgeable, reliable, and trustworthy, they are more likely to engage with you, seek your advice, and ultimately make purchases.

2. Establishing Authority and Expertise:
Personal branding allows you to position yourself as an authority and expert in your field. By showcasing your knowledge, skills, and experience, you demonstrate your competence and authority, earning the respect and admiration of both customers and colleagues.

3. Fostering Meaningful Connections:
Personal branding enables you to connect with customers on a deeper level beyond transactional interactions. By sharing your story, values, and personality, you humanize your brand and forge authentic connections that resonate with customers on an emotional level.

4. Driving Customer Loyalty and Advocacy:
A compelling personal brand fosters customer loyalty and advocacy. When customers feel a personal connection with you, they are more likely to become repeat buyers, recommend your services to others, and advocate for your brand both online and offline.

5. Standing Out in a Crowded Market:
In a crowded marketplace, personal branding helps you stand out from the competition. By defining what makes you unique and communicating it effectively, you create a distinct identity that sets you apart and attracts customers who resonate with your values and personality.

6. Enhancing Career Opportunities:

Personal branding can open doors to new career opportunities and advancement in the retail sales industry. When you establish yourself as a thought leader and influencer in your field, you become a magnet for career opportunities, networking connections, and professional growth.

7. Adapting to Changing Market Dynamics:
In today's rapidly evolving retail landscape, personal branding enables you to adapt to changing market dynamics and consumer preferences. By staying agile and responsive, you can pivot your brand messaging, offerings, and strategies to meet evolving customer needs and stay ahead of the curve.

8. Creating Long-Term Value:
Ultimately, personal branding is about creating long-term value for yourself and your customers. By investing in your personal brand, you lay the foundation for sustained success, growth, and fulfillment in your career as a retail sales professional.

In conclusion, personal branding is not just a vanity exercise — it's a strategic imperative for retail sales professionals seeking to differentiate themselves, build trust, and drive success in a competitive marketplace. By understanding the relevance of personal branding and leveraging it effectively, you can establish a strong presence, foster meaningful connections, and achieve your goals in the dynamic world of retail sales.

Chapter: Building Your Online Presence and Reputation

In today's digital age, your online presence is often the first impression you make on potential customers and employers. This chapter explores strategies for building a strong online presence and reputation as a retail sales professional, empowering you to showcase your expertise, connect with your audience, and unlock new opportunities for success.

1. Create a Professional Profile:

Start by creating a professional profile on LinkedIn, the leading platform for professional networking. Complete your profile with a professional photo, a compelling headline, and a summary that highlights your skills, experience, and accomplishments. Ensure that your profile is up-to-date and showcases your expertise in retail sales.

2. Share Valuable Content:

Share valuable content related to retail sales on your LinkedIn profile and other social media platforms. This could include industry insights, sales tips, product reviews, or success stories. By sharing your knowledge and expertise, you demonstrate your credibility and position yourself as a thought leader in your field.

3. Engage with Your Network:

Engage with your network by commenting on posts, sharing articles, and participating in industry discussions. Actively engage with peers, colleagues, and industry influencers to build meaningful connections and expand your professional network. By contributing to the conversation, you demonstrate your expertise and increase your visibility within the industry.

4. Showcase Your Achievements:

Highlight your achievements and successes as a retail sales professional on your online profiles. This could include exceeding sales targets, winning awards, or receiving positive feedback from customers or colleagues. By showcasing your accomplishments, you reinforce your reputation as a high-performing sales professional and attract opportunities for recognition and advancement.

5. Seek Recommendations and Endorsements:

Request recommendations and endorsements from colleagues, supervisors, and satisfied customers to strengthen your online reputation. Genuine testimonials from others validate your skills and expertise and provide social proof of your capabilities as a retail sales professional. Display these recommendations prominently on your online profiles to build credibility and trust with potential employers and customers.

6. Participate in Online Communities:

Join online communities and forums related to retail sales to connect with like-minded professionals and exchange insights and ideas. Participate in discussions, ask questions, and share your expertise to establish yourself as a valuable contributor to the community. By actively participating in online communities, you expand your network and position yourself as an authority in your field.

7. Monitor Your Online Presence:

Regularly monitor your online presence to ensure that it accurately reflects your professional brand. Google yourself to see what information comes up and take steps to manage your online reputation effectively. Address any negative or inaccurate information promptly and proactively manage your privacy settings to control what information is visible to others.

8. Stay Authentic and Consistent:

Above all, stay authentic and consistent in your online presence. Let your personality shine through in your interactions and content, and ensure that your online persona aligns with your offline reputation. By being genuine and consistent, you build trust and credibility with your audience, strengthening your online reputation as a retail sales professional.

In conclusion, building a strong online presence and reputation is essential for success in today's digital world. By leveraging online platforms, sharing valuable content, engaging with your network, and showcasing your achievements, you can establish yourself as a trusted authority in retail sales and unlock new opportunities for growth and advancement in your career.

Chapter: Networking and Building Relationships within the Retail Industry

In the dynamic and interconnected world of retail, building and nurturing relationships is paramount for success. This chapter explores the importance of networking and provides actionable strategies for retail professionals to effectively build relationships within the industry, fostering opportunities for collaboration, growth, and advancement.

1. Recognizing the Importance of Networking:

Networking is more than just exchanging business cards — it's about building meaningful connections with others in the industry. Whether you're seeking career opportunities, business partnerships, or industry insights, networking allows you to tap into a wealth of resources, expertise, and support within your professional community.

2. Engaging in Industry Events and Conferences:

Industry events and conferences provide invaluable opportunities for networking and professional development. Attend trade shows, seminars, and networking events within the retail industry to connect with peers, industry leaders, and potential collaborators. Actively participate in discussions, ask questions, and exchange contact information to build lasting relationships with others in the industry.

3. Leveraging Online Platforms and Communities:

Online platforms such as LinkedIn, industry forums, and professional networking groups offer additional avenues for networking within the retail industry. Join relevant groups and communities, participate in discussions, and connect with professionals who share your interests and goals. Engage with others by sharing insights, asking questions, and offering support to foster meaningful connections online.

4. Cultivating Relationships with Colleagues and Peers:

Building relationships with colleagues and peers within your organization and across the industry is essential for career growth and professional development. Take the time to get to know your coworkers, collaborate on projects, and offer assistance whenever possible. By fostering a supportive and collaborative work environment, you can build strong relationships that benefit both your career and the organization as a whole.

5. Seeking Mentorship and Guidance:

Mentorship is a valuable resource for personal and professional growth within the retail industry. Seek out mentors who have experience and expertise in your field, and learn from their insights, advice, and guidance. A mentor can provide valuable perspective, support, and encouragement as you navigate your career path and overcome challenges along the way.

6. Providing Value and Building Trust:

Networking is not just about what you can gain—it's also about what you can contribute. Look for opportunities to provide value to others within the industry, whether through sharing knowledge, offering assistance, or making introductions. By demonstrating your expertise, reliability, and integrity, you build trust and credibility with your network, strengthening your relationships over time.

7. Following Up and Staying Connected:

After making initial connections, it's important to follow up and stay connected with your network regularly. Send personalized follow-up emails or messages to express appreciation for the conversation and reaffirm your interest in staying in touch. Stay engaged with your network by sharing updates, offering assistance, and reaching out periodically to nurture your relationships.

8. Embracing Diversity and Inclusion:

Embrace diversity and inclusion in your networking efforts by seeking out connections from diverse backgrounds, experiences, and perspectives. Building a diverse network enriches your own understanding, expands your opportunities, and fosters a culture of inclusivity within the industry. Be open-minded, respectful, and inclusive in your interactions with others, and strive to create a welcoming and supportive community for all.

In conclusion, networking is a fundamental skill for success in the retail industry. By actively engaging in networking opportunities, cultivating relationships with peers and colleagues, and providing value to others, you can build a strong network of support, collaboration, and growth within the industry. Networking isn't just about advancing your own career—it's about contributing to the collective success of the retail community and fostering a culture of collaboration and innovation for the future.

Chapter: Strategies for Career Advancement and Continued Learning

In the dynamic and competitive field of retail, ongoing learning and professional development are essential for career advancement and personal growth. This chapter explores actionable strategies for retail professionals to propel their careers forward, acquire new skills, and stay ahead of the curve in an ever-evolving industry.

1. Set Clear Goals and Objectives:

Define your career goals and aspirations, and develop a roadmap for achieving them. Whether it's advancing to a higher position, transitioning to a new role, or expanding your skill set, clarity of purpose will guide your actions and decisions towards career advancement.

2. Invest in Continuous Learning:

Commit to lifelong learning and professional development to stay relevant and competitive in the retail industry. Pursue opportunities for formal education, certifications, workshops, and seminars that enhance your skills and knowledge. Embrace a growth mindset and seek out new challenges and learning experiences to expand your capabilities.

3. Seek Feedback and Mentorship:

Seek feedback from peers, supervisors, and mentors to gain insights into your strengths and areas for improvement. Actively solicit feedback on your performance, seek advice from experienced professionals, and leverage mentorship opportunities to accelerate your growth and development.

4. Take on New Challenges and Responsibilities:

Volunteer for projects, assignments, and initiatives that stretch your abilities and broaden your experience. Embrace new challenges and responsibilities, even if they push you outside your comfort zone. Taking initiative and demonstrating a willingness to learn and grow will position you as a proactive and valuable asset to your organization.

5. Build a Strong Professional Network:

Network strategically within the retail industry to expand your circle of influence and uncover new opportunities for career advancement. Attend industry events, join professional associations, and connect with peers, mentors, and industry leaders. Cultivate relationships with others in the industry, and leverage your network for advice, support, and career opportunities.

6. Develop Leadership Skills:

Develop leadership skills that are essential for career advancement in retail. Take on leadership roles within your organization, mentor junior colleagues, and demonstrate your ability to inspire, motivate, and lead others. Invest in leadership training and development programs to hone your skills and prepare for future leadership opportunities.

7. Stay Current with Industry Trends:

Stay informed about industry trends, innovations, and best practices to remain relevant in the rapidly evolving retail landscape. Follow industry publications, attend conferences, and participate in webinars to stay abreast of emerging trends and developments. Being knowledgeable about industry trends demonstrates your commitment to staying ahead of the curve and adds value to your organization.

8. Embrace Change and Adaptability:

In today's fast-paced retail environment, adaptability is key to success. Embrace change as an opportunity for growth and innovation, and be flexible in your approach to new challenges and opportunities. Demonstrate your ability to adapt to changing circumstances, pivot quickly, and thrive in dynamic environments to position yourself for career advancement.

9. Cultivate a Personal Brand:

Developing a strong personal brand can differentiate you from your peers and enhance your visibility and credibility within the industry. Showcase your expertise, accomplishments, and unique value proposition through online and offline channels. By building a compelling personal brand, you can attract new opportunities, establish yourself as a thought leader, and advance your career in the retail industry.

In conclusion, career advancement in the retail industry requires a proactive approach to learning, growth, and development. By setting clear goals, investing in continuous learning, seeking feedback and mentorship, embracing new challenges, and building a strong network, you can position yourself for success and unlock new opportunities for advancement in your retail career.

Conclusion: Recap of Key Concepts Covered in the Book

Throughout this book, we have explored a diverse range of topics aimed at equipping retail sales professionals with the knowledge, skills, and strategies needed to excel in their careers. Let's recap the key concepts covered:

1. Fundamentals of Retail Sales:
We began by laying the foundation with an overview of the fundamentals of retail sales, including understanding customer needs, effective communication, and sales techniques.

2. Techniques for Closing Sales and Securing Customer Loyalty:

We delved into techniques for closing sales and fostering customer loyalty, exploring strategies such as active listening, objection handling, and relationship-building.

3. Providing Exceptional Customer Service:
Customer service emerged as a cornerstone of retail success, with a focus on delivering exceptional experiences, exceeding expectations, and building lasting relationships with customers.

4. Understanding the Importance of Customer Service in Retail:
We examined the significance of customer service in retail, highlighting its impact on customer satisfaction, loyalty, and advocacy, and its role in driving business growth.

5. Strategies for Delivering Outstanding Customer Experiences:
Strategies for delivering outstanding customer experiences were explored, emphasizing the importance of personalization, empathy, and responsiveness in creating memorable interactions.

6. Handling Customer Complaints and Turning Them into Opportunities:
We addressed the art of handling customer complaints effectively, transforming challenges into opportunities for service recovery, learning, and relationship-building.

7. Building Long-Term Relationships with Customers:
The importance of building long-term relationships with customers was emphasized, with a focus on trust, authenticity, and ongoing engagement beyond transactional interactions.

8. Harnessing the Power of Data and Analytics:

We introduced the concept of retail analytics, exploring its applications in understanding customer preferences, optimizing operations, and driving informed decision-making.

9. Introduction to Retail Analytics:
The chapter provided an overview of retail analytics, its significance, and key applications in areas such as customer segmentation, inventory management, and pricing optimization.

10. Using Data to Understand Customer Preferences and Behavior:
We explored the role of data in understanding customer preferences and behavior, leveraging analytics to personalize experiences, predict trends, and drive strategic decision-making.

11. Implementing Data-Driven Strategies for Sales Optimization:
Strategies for implementing data-driven strategies for sales optimization were examined, including demand forecasting, pricing optimization, and personalized marketing.

12. Leveraging Analytics to Forecast Trends and Improve Decision-Making:
The chapter highlighted the importance of leveraging analytics to forecast trends, anticipate market dynamics, and make informed decisions to stay ahead of the curve.

13. Developing Your Personal Brand as a Retail Sales Professional:
Personal branding emerged as a critical aspect of career development, empowering professionals to differentiate themselves, showcase their expertise, and build meaningful connections within the industry.

14. Building Your Online Presence and Reputation:
We explored strategies for building a strong online presence and reputation, including creating professional profiles, sharing valuable content, and engaging with peers and industry influencers.

15. Networking and Building Relationships within the Retail Industry:
The chapter emphasized the importance of networking and relationship-building in retail, providing strategies for expanding professional networks, cultivating meaningful connections, and fostering collaboration.

16. Strategies for Career Advancement and Continued Learning:
Finally, we examined actionable strategies for career advancement and continued learning, including setting goals, investing in continuous learning, seeking feedback, and embracing new challenges.

In conclusion, this book has provided a comprehensive toolkit for retail sales professionals to excel in their careers, from mastering sales techniques and delivering exceptional customer service to leveraging data and analytics for strategic decision-making and personal growth. By applying the concepts and strategies covered in this book, retail professionals can navigate the complexities of the retail landscape, drive business success, and achieve their career aspirations.

Chapter: Encouragement and Inspiration for Retail Sales Professionals

In the fast-paced world of retail sales, staying motivated and inspired is essential for success and personal fulfillment. This chapter serves as a source of encouragement and inspiration for retail sales professionals, offering insights, advice, and affirmations to fuel their passion and drive their career forward.

1. Embrace the Power of Positivity:

Maintaining a positive attitude is crucial in the face of challenges and setbacks. Embrace a mindset of positivity and optimism, focusing on solutions rather than dwelling on problems. Remember that every obstacle is an opportunity for growth and learning, and approach each day with enthusiasm and determination.

2. Celebrate Your Achievements:

Take time to celebrate your accomplishments, no matter how small. Recognize and acknowledge your successes, whether it's reaching sales targets, receiving positive feedback from customers, or overcoming obstacles. Celebrating your achievements boosts morale, reinforces your confidence, and motivates you to strive for even greater heights.

3. Embrace Continuous Learning and Growth:

Commit to lifelong learning and personal development to fuel your growth and advancement in your career. Embrace new challenges, seek out learning opportunities, and continuously expand your skills and knowledge. Remember that growth happens outside your comfort zone, so don't be afraid to push yourself and pursue new experiences.

4. Find Purpose in Your Work:

Connect with the deeper purpose behind your work in retail sales. Whether it's helping customers solve problems, making a positive impact on their lives, or contributing to your team's success, find meaning and fulfillment in the work you do. When you align your work with your values and purpose, you'll feel more motivated and inspired to give your best every day.

5. Cultivate Resilience in the Face of Challenges:

Resilience is the ability to bounce back from setbacks and adversity. Cultivate resilience by developing coping mechanisms, practicing self-care, and seeking support from colleagues, friends, and mentors. Remember that setbacks are temporary, and every challenge you overcome makes you stronger and more resilient in the long run.

6. Surround Yourself with Supportive Peers:

Surround yourself with colleagues who inspire and support you in your journey. Build a network of peers who share your values, aspirations, and passion for excellence. Lean on each other for encouragement, advice, and camaraderie, and celebrate each other's successes along the way.

7. Stay Connected to Your Why:

Stay connected to the reasons why you chose a career in retail sales. Whether it's your love for helping people, your passion for the products you sell, or your desire to make a difference in your community, keep your why front and center in your mind. When you stay connected to your purpose, you'll find renewed energy and motivation to overcome any obstacles you encounter.

8. Practice Self-Compassion and Self-Care:

Be kind to yourself and prioritize self-care in your daily life. Practice self-compassion by treating yourself with the same kindness and understanding you would offer to a friend. Take breaks when you need them, prioritize your physical and mental well-being, and recharge your batteries regularly to avoid burnout.

9. Visualize Your Success:

Visualize yourself achieving your goals and living your dreams. Create a clear mental image of what success looks and feels like for you, and use it as motivation to keep pushing forward, even when the going gets tough. Visualization is a powerful tool for manifesting your desires and turning your dreams into reality.

10. Remember That Every Day Is a Fresh Start:

Finally, remember that every day is a new opportunity to start afresh. Leave behind any mistakes or disappointments from yesterday and approach each day with renewed optimism and determination. Every moment is a chance to make a positive impact, so make the most of it and embrace the journey with an open heart and mind.

In conclusion, as a retail sales professional, you have the power to create your own success and make a meaningful difference in the lives of others. Stay motivated, inspired, and committed to your goals, and remember that with passion, perseverance, and positivity, anything is possible. You have what it takes to achieve greatness in your career, so go forth with confidence and make your dreams a reality.

Chapter: Looking Ahead: Embracing Change and Continuous Improvement in Retail Sales

The retail landscape is constantly evolving, driven by technological advancements, shifting consumer behaviors, and emerging market trends. In this final chapter, we explore the importance of embracing change and committing to continuous improvement as retail sales professionals, empowering us to thrive in an ever-changing environment.

1. Embracing Change as an Opportunity:

Change is inevitable in the retail industry, and embracing it is essential for growth and adaptation. Instead of resisting change, view it as an opportunity for innovation, learning, and growth. Stay open-minded and flexible in the face of change, and approach new challenges with curiosity and enthusiasm.

2. Adopting a Growth Mindset:

Cultivate a growth mindset that embraces challenges and sees failures as opportunities for learning and improvement. Believe in your ability to develop new skills, overcome obstacles, and adapt to change. By adopting a growth mindset, you empower yourself to thrive in dynamic and uncertain environments.

3. Emphasizing Continuous Learning and Development:

Commit to lifelong learning and personal development to stay relevant and competitive in the retail industry. Stay informed about emerging trends, technologies, and best practices through books, courses, seminars, and industry events. Invest in acquiring new skills and knowledge that will enhance your effectiveness as a retail sales professional.

4. Leveraging Technology for Innovation:

Technology is transforming the retail landscape, offering new opportunities for innovation and efficiency. Embrace technology as a tool to enhance your sales processes, improve customer experiences, and gain insights into consumer behavior. Stay informed about emerging technologies such as artificial intelligence, augmented reality, and predictive analytics, and explore how they can benefit your work in retail sales.

5. Prioritizing Customer-Centricity:

In an increasingly competitive market, prioritizing customer-centricity is essential for success. Place the needs and preferences of your customers at the center of everything you do, and strive to deliver personalized, seamless experiences that exceed their expectations. Listen to customer feedback, anticipate their needs, and tailor your approach accordingly to build lasting relationships and drive loyalty.

6. Embracing Diversity and Inclusion:

Diversity and inclusion are integral to fostering innovation, creativity, and collaboration in the retail industry. Embrace diversity in all its forms, including race, gender, age, and background, and create an inclusive work environment where everyone feels valued and respected. Celebrate the unique perspectives and contributions of each individual, and leverage the power of diversity to drive positive change and innovation.

7. Nurturing a Culture of Collaboration:

Collaboration is key to navigating the complexities of the retail landscape and driving collective success. Foster a culture of collaboration within your organization by promoting teamwork, communication, and knowledge-sharing. Break down silos between departments, encourage cross-functional collaboration, and recognize and celebrate team achievements to create a cohesive and supportive work environment.

8. Adapting to Evolving Consumer Behaviors:

Consumer behaviors and preferences are constantly evolving, influenced by factors such as technology, social trends, and economic conditions. Stay attuned to changes in consumer behavior and adapt your sales strategies accordingly. Be proactive in anticipating emerging trends and aligning your offerings and marketing efforts to meet evolving customer needs and expectations.

9. Setting Goals and Monitoring Progress:

Set clear, achievable goals for yourself and your team, and regularly monitor progress towards them. Break down larger goals into smaller, actionable steps, and celebrate milestones along the way. Use data and analytics to track performance, identify areas for improvement, and make informed decisions that drive progress towards your objectives.

10. Cultivating Resilience and Adaptability:

Resilience and adaptability are essential qualities for navigating uncertainty and thriving in a constantly changing environment. Develop resilience by building coping mechanisms, practicing self-care, and seeking support from colleagues, friends, and mentors. Embrace change with a spirit of adaptability and flexibility, and approach challenges as opportunities for growth and learning.

In conclusion, the future of retail sales is bright, filled with opportunities for innovation, growth, and success. By embracing change, committing to continuous improvement, and staying customer-centric, we can navigate the complexities of the retail landscape with confidence and resilience. Let us embrace the journey ahead with optimism, curiosity, and a commitment to excellence in all that we do.

Appendix: Additional Resources for Further Learning

Continuing your learning journey beyond this book is essential for professional growth and development in the field of retail sales. Here are some additional resources to explore for further learning:

1. Books:

"To Sell Is Human: The Surprising Truth About Moving Others" by Daniel H. Pink
"Influence: The Psychology of Persuasion" by Robert B. Cialdini
"The Challenger Sale: Taking Control of the Customer Conversation" by Matthew Dixon and Brent Adamson
"Customer Satisfaction Is Worthless, Customer Loyalty Is Priceless" by Jeffrey Gitomer
"The Retail Doctor's Guide to Growing Your Business: A Step-by-Step Approach to Quickly Diagnose, Treat, and Cure" by Bob Phibbs

2. Online Courses:

LinkedIn Learning: Offers a variety of courses on retail sales, customer service, and leadership skills.

Udemy: Provides courses on sales techniques, retail management, and customer experience optimization.
Coursera: Features courses from top universities and institutions on topics such as marketing, consumer behavior, and data analytics.

3. Industry Publications:

Retail Dive: Provides news, insights, and analysis on the retail industry.
NRF (National Retail Federation) Blog: Offers articles, research reports, and thought leadership pieces on retail trends and best practices.
Harvard Business Review: Publishes articles and case studies on sales, marketing, and customer experience in the retail sector.

4. Podcasts:

The Modern Retail Podcast: Explores trends, challenges, and innovations in the retail industry through interviews with industry experts and thought leaders.
The Sales Evangelist Podcast: Offers tips, strategies, and insights for improving sales performance and building customer relationships.
Retail Gets Real: Hosted by the National Retail Federation, this podcast features interviews with retail executives and entrepreneurs sharing their experiences and perspectives on the industry.

5. Professional Associations:

National Retail Federation (NRF): Provides resources, events, and networking opportunities for retail professionals.
Retail Industry Leaders Association (RILA): Offers advocacy, research, and networking opportunities for retail leaders and executives.

Sales & Marketing Executives International (SMEI): Provides training, certifications, and networking events for sales and marketing professionals.

6. Online Communities:

RetailWire: A community for retail professionals to discuss industry trends, challenges, and best practices.

Sales Hacker: A community for sales professionals to share strategies, tools, and resources for driving sales success.

LinkedIn Groups: Join relevant LinkedIn groups focused on retail sales, customer experience, and industry-specific topics to connect with peers and share insights.

7. Webinars and Events:

Attend webinars and events hosted by industry organizations, professional associations, and thought leaders to stay informed about the latest trends and innovations in retail sales.

Look for local meetups, networking events, and conferences in your area to connect with fellow professionals and learn from industry experts.

Remember: Continuously investing in your learning and development is key to staying competitive and advancing your career in the dynamic field of retail sales. Explore these resources, seek out opportunities for growth, and never stop striving for excellence in your profession.

Glossary of Retail Sales Terminology

Understanding the terminology used in retail sales is essential for effective communication and success in the industry. Here's a glossary of common terms and phrases you may encounter:

1. Upselling:
Encouraging customers to purchase additional or higher-priced items or services than originally intended.

2. Cross-selling:
Suggesting complementary or related products to customers to enhance their purchase and increase sales.

3. Average Transaction Value (ATV):
The average amount spent by a customer during a single transaction or visit to a retail store.

4. Conversion Rate:
The percentage of visitors to a store or website who make a purchase.

5. Gross Margin:
The difference between revenue and the cost of goods sold, expressed as a percentage of revenue.

6. Inventory Turnover:
The number of times inventory is sold and replaced within a specific period, typically a year.

7. Loss Prevention:
Strategies and measures implemented to prevent theft, fraud, and shrinkage in retail stores.

8. Point of Sale (POS) System:
A computerized system used to process transactions, manage inventory, and track sales in retail stores.

9. Customer Relationship Management (CRM):
Software and strategies used to manage interactions and relationships with customers, including sales, marketing, and service activities.

10. Sales Funnel:
A visual representation of the customer journey, from initial awareness to purchase, used to track and optimize sales performance.

11. Lead Generation:
The process of identifying and attracting potential customers or leads for a product or service.

12. Cold Calling:
Making unsolicited phone calls or visits to prospective customers to generate sales leads or appointments.

13. Commission:
A percentage of sales revenue or a fixed amount paid to salespeople as compensation for their sales performance.

14. KPI (Key Performance Indicator):

Metrics used to evaluate the performance and effectiveness of sales activities and strategies.

15. Merchandising:
The planning, organization, and presentation of products in retail stores to maximize sales and customer satisfaction.

16. Sales Forecasting:
Predicting future sales trends and outcomes based on historical data, market analysis, and other factors.

17. Customer Segmentation:
Dividing customers into distinct groups based on demographics, behavior, or other characteristics for targeted marketing and sales strategies.

18. Return on Investment (ROI):
The ratio of net profit to the cost of an investment, used to evaluate the profitability of sales and marketing initiatives.

19. Sales Promotion:
Marketing activities designed to stimulate sales, such as discounts, coupons, contests, and special offers.

20. After-Sales Service:
Support and assistance provided to customers after they have made a purchase, including installation, maintenance, and troubleshooting.

Remember: This glossary serves as a reference guide to help you navigate the terminology commonly used in retail sales. Continuously expanding your knowledge of these terms and concepts will enhance your effectiveness and success in the field.

www.ingramcontent.com/pod-product-compliance
Lightning Source LLC
Chambersburg PA
CBHW052202220526
45471CB00004B/1781